PLANTED

SIT, STAND, AND WALK WITH JESUS

A STUDY OF PSALM 1:1-3

ANNIE PAJCIC

Creating Art through God's Word
www.thouartexalted.com

TABLE OF CONTENTS

WEEKS OF STUDY

LEADER AND VIEWER'S GUIDE

Let me begin by saying THANK YOU for purchasing PLANTED and being a part of our study together. Whether you are doing this Bible study alone or with a group of friends, I hope this guide will be helpful to you.

PLANTED is a ten-week Bible study divided into three sections: Sit, Stand, and Walk with Jesus. The first week's lesson, also known as the Introductory Session, will give you the overall theme of Planted. If you choose to watch the **teaching videos,** the Introductory Video will be watched **before** you begin the first lesson. Each session following will have an optional teaching video after the lesson has been completed. You can download these videos at **www.thouartexalted.com/planted/ teaching videos.** The lessons are divided into five segments of homework that should take no longer than 30 minutes a day. If you are a small group leader, have a highlighter nearby to highlight the questions that meant most to you during your quiet times. This will be a quick reference for discussion when leading your small group.

I believe the purpose of a small group is to fellowship with one another and to grow in the knowledge of God's Word. I love small groups because they build friendships that are rooted deep in the Truth. Small groups are intended for allowing the Word to penetrate into the realness of our lives. After leading small groups for years, I have some TIPS to share with you:

1. Keep track of TIME.

I take the time allotted for my small group discussions and divide by five, the days of homework. For example: If you have 50 minutes to discuss your homework, then allow 10 minutes per day and use your highlighted questions to be your main focus. Ask your group if one question stood out among the others and how God used that question to make a difference in their life. Remember to always look at your watch and keep the conversation going. If you have time at the end, you can always go back to look at a question.

2. Keep conversation on TOPIC.

Women can be easily distracted and quickly get off course. (Watch out for the section when I talk about window shopping!) Your job is to keep everyone on track. Ask the Holy Spirit to give you gentleness as you steer the conversation back on topic.

3. Keep TALKY people to a minimum.

I realize not everyone wants to share in a small group. Try to allow a chance for everyone to participate and not have one lady rule the conversation. If you have this situation, you might want to speak to her in private and encourage her to allow others to share their answers. Be sensitive to the needs of others and ask God for wisdom.

4. Allow TIME to prepare.

As a leader, be prepared to facilitate your small group. This means … doing your homework! You can't lead if you haven't taken time to sit with the Lord and study PLANTED.

5. TAKE time to PRAY with and for your small group.

This is one of the most important aspects of your group. I would encourage you to take prayer requests at the end of each discussion time and emphasize the confidentiality of the group. Prayers and discussions are personal and should not be taken outside your small group.

This is not a complete list of "how-to" lead a small group by any means, but hopefully I hit a few good points! Remember to be real. Be yourself. Be inviting. Allow the Holy Spirit to lead you as you have the privilege to lead your small group. And, if you ever have any questions, please email me at apajcic@comcast.net.

I am praying for you, sweet friend.

It is with great delight that God has challenged and inspired me to write and design **PLANTED**. Writing Bible studies is not a foreign concept to me, but my audience is usually under five feet tall! Studying God's Word is similar to that of singing to a child. God believes our voices are beautiful and loves the fact we are singing, even when we think we can't carry a tune! My prayer for ALL of us is not that we would be able to carry a tune, but that we would **carry** our concerns, our hopes, our dreams, our expectations, our disappointments, our reality … down to God's river where the **power** of Christ can wash over them.

PLANTED will take us to the riverbank where we will have conversations with God. We will learn what it means to be blessed by Him and how our lives should resemble the tree described in Psalm 1:2-3. **PLANTED** will teach us the importance of taking time out of our busy lives just to **sit** with God. We will look at ways to study His Word and be reminded to **stand** on the promises in Scripture. We will learn what it means to be transformed by Christ as we **walk** with Him during days of joy and in moments of sorrow. We will find He is **always** there to meet us. Even if we fail, He is right there to pick us up and carry us through.

This reminds me of a day in college at SMU when I was studying for exams in one of Dallas' many beautiful parks. My eye was drawn to a young mom and her child. Obviously, I was more interested in them than studying French! She was strolling her daughter down the sidewalk when it became very clear that the two-year-old wanted **out**. I could see the struggle as the child demanded that SHE wanted to push the stroller. Her mom, with great tenderness and compassion, allowed the child to steer. The little girl promptly steered the stroller right off the sidewalk and onto the grass. She did not have enough power or vision to see that her "ride" was stuck. The mother, with more patience than I would have had, sweetly picked up the frustrated child and calmly put her back into the stroller. This scenario repeated itself a couple of times. Each time, the mother demonstrated gentle grace, picking up her daughter, giving her a hug, and placing her right back where she belonged.

Aren't we just like this? Sometimes, I want to be in control and steer my own life, too! But God can see and steer with a strength and a perspective that I cannot. Even when we don't understand why we are stuck and try to demand our own way, He, with gentle compassion and grace, **picks us up**. He tells us how much He loves us and sits us back where we belong. Together, we move forward in the right direction. C'est bon!

PLANTED is about moving us in the right direction. It's about giving God the wheel and letting Him plant us where we need to be—so we can grow UP into the strong tree described in Psalm 1:2-3. When our roots are deeply **PLANTED** into the fellowship, the love, the grace, and the Word of God, we can't help but become like a beautiful strong tree with purpose. Our leaves will not wither under the stresses and storms of life, our fruit will be abundant, and our lives will prosper. It's a promise on which we can **stand**.

PLANTED is divided into three sections—**sitting**, **standing,** and **walking** with Jesus. We have to **SIT** in God's presence in order to **STAND** on His promises preparing us to **WALK** in His purposes. Each week includes five daily discussions that should take no longer than 30 minutes to complete. You will learn:

- That you are PURPOSELY PLANTED by God.
- What it looks like to SIT at the feet of Jesus—being PATIENT, PRAYERFUL, and full of PRAISE.
- How to STAND on His PROMISES and PERSEVERE when the pressures of life blow the leaves off of your limbs.
- How your FRUIT will be abundant and your life will be PROSPEROUS when you remain connected to God.

In order to grow, you have to do your part. You can't expect to grow while demanding to steer your own stroller. It is your choice whether you want to join Him at the river. Take some time today to read Psalm 1:1-3. Get familiar with the verses because they will be your foundation for the next 10 weeks. Please know that I am praying for you. I thank God for you. I am praying for all of us to be **PLANTED**.

In the mighty name of Jesus,
Annie

Viewer Guide: Introduction

God's Love is our Unfailing Anchor

"We must pay MORE careful ATTENTION, therefore to what we have HEARD so that we do not DRIFT away."

Hebrews 2:1

Welcome to PLANTED: Sitting in His Presence, Standing on His Promises, and Walking in His Purposes! We are called to be TREES of high standing before the Lord. Today we will focus on Hebrews 2:1. We are called to pay MORE careful attention to Jesus. Let's get started!

1. "Blessed is the man who does not _____ in the counsel of the wicked or _____ in the way of sinners or _____ in the seat of mockers. But his DELIGHT is in the law of the Lord, and on his law, he _____ day and night. He is like a TREE _____ by streams of water which yields its FRUIT in season and whose LEAF does not wither, whatever he does PROSPERS."

Psalm 1:1-3, NIV

2. Psalm One compares and contrasts two characters. We find they are ALIKE because they are _____ and breathing, and they have the right to make a _____. They are different because one is being BLESSED, and one is not being BLESSED. One is anchored, and one is not.

* TO WHAT SHOULD WE PAY MORE ATTENTION?

3. **PLANTED** means: placed _____ so it can grow, established, fixed in a place.

4. In Hebrews 2:1, God wants us to pay _____ careful attention to.
Paying **more** careful attention to can also be translated as: _____.

* WHAT HAVE WE HEARD?

5. What should we pay more careful attention to? We need to pay more careful attention to what we have _____, _____ Jesus is, and _____ to follow Him.

Hebrews 2:1, The Message
"It is CRITICAL to keep a firm grip on what we have heard so we do not drift off."

*TO WHAT ARE WE DRIFTING OFF?

6. When we "mix" Jesus into our lives, He becomes a simple _____ or a substitute. Jesus doesn't want to be a simple ingredient in our life, He wants to be the _____. He wants ALL of our life.

7. What are the INSTRUCTIONS in Psalm 1:1-3? We need to _____ and delight on the law of God, to read Scripture, and to SIT on it. What is the result? We will be like a _____ PLANTED.

8. Do you think you have drifted too far? Here is the PROMISE: No one can drift too far beyond the extended arms of His _____.

9. Isaiah 54:10 says: "'Though the mountains be shaken and the hills removed, yet my unfailing love for you will not be _____ nor my covenant of peace removed,' says the Lord, who has _____ on YOU."

10. We have a **CHOICE** to make. We can either choose to drift off by the waves of the world, or we can choose to be _____. Jesus is **always** there to stretch out His hand and rescue us.
God's love is our unfailing anchor.

NOTES:

Key to Lesson: Walk, Stand, Sit, Meditate, Planted, Alive, Choice, Purposefully, More, Beware, Heard, Who, How, Ingredient, Recipe, Meditate, Tree, Love, Shaken, Compassion, Planted

Video sessions are available for download at www.thouartexalted.com/PLANTED ~ teaching videos   7

I was nervous from the start. I loved her dearly, but I had never spent the night alone with my grandmother in a hotel room. She was 86 years old, and who would have known her nightly routines? Women are funny about them, you know? I have my own quirky regimen … wash face, brush teeth, take out contacts, and put on glasses to be able to see—anything.

Iyii, pronounced "I~I", was her name. I assume the beloved naming came from the fact that my oldest sister could not pronounce her last name, Ira. Iyii was a beautiful woman of southern proportion. She was a lady of first class. Although born in Maine, she spent most of her life in the South sipping sweet tea and living under moss-covered oak trees. On the outside, she was always "finished." That's a good southern term. Her purse always matched her shoes, and let's not forget, her lipstick. On the inside, she was **pure** genuine. Everyone knew Iyii was as good as they come. She taught Sunday School and never missed a Wednesday night supper at church. She offered the hospitality of sweet conversation and always had time to listen to the tales of her grandchildren. Her favorite inventions were the ballpoint pen, the hot dog, and air conditioning. Born in 1905, she could have written the Samantha series for the American Girl Doll. ®

As we got ready for bed, she smiled at me and said, "Annie, I am going to take out my hearing aids, so I won't be able to hear you."

"That's fine Iyii," I replied, "because when I take off my glasses, I won't be able to see you."

We both laughed and turned out the lights.

What was I worried about anyway? How many grandchildren get the opportunity to spend the night with their grandmother? This was a blessing just to be with her. Until … .

"Annie!"

My heart zipped into super speed. "Is something wrong? How can I help?" I asked.

"Oh Annie, I forgot to pray."

The moment was suspended in time as I watched my grandmother get out of her bed, in the dark, kneel beside her mattress, and pray. And pray. And **pray.**

Time seemed to soften. My fear of staying alone with her was removed and replaced with a holy snapshot into the spiritual life of my Iyii.

> She knew her Shepherd, and He knew her prayers.
> She knew her Lord, and He called her by name.
> She knew that not one day could go by without going on her knees in worship.

She was **PLANTED.**

The idea for this book **sprouted** (yes, I do have the license to be corny!) when I was asked to speak at a women's luncheon in Jacksonville. The team of women had already decided the title would be, *The Truth about Trees,* from the passage in first Psalm.

> *"Blessed is the man*
> *who does not WALK in the counsel of the wicked*
> *or STAND in the way of sinners*
> *or SIT in the seat of mockers.*
>
> *But his DELIGHT is in the law of the Lord,*
> *and on his law, he MEDITATES day and night.*
> *He is like a TREE PLANTED by streams of water*
> *which yields its FRUIT in season*
> *and whose LEAF does not wither,*
> *whatever he does PROSPERS."*
>
> *Psalm 1:1-3*

Not only was I excited, but I was also familiar with these verses, thanks to Stormie Omartian. While in the airport, I had bought her book, *The Power of a Praying Wife.* [1] Following wife her instructions, I had prayed these verses over my husband. It went something like this:

> *Oh Lord, I pray Curry would not walk in the counsel of the wicked or stand in the way of sinners, or sit in the seat of mockers, but he would delight in Your Truth and meditate on it, study it, remember it, and use it. I pray he would be like this tree standing firm against the winds of this world. I pray he would not be tempted by evil, but stay firm in Your promises. Lord, I pray that whatever he does would prosper today, not for his name's sake, but for the glory of Your Name.*

I also prayed this passage over my four children as a **blessing**:

> *Oh Lord, I pray _____(insert name) would not walk, stand, or sit in places where he/she should not. I pray _____'s delight and desire would be to serve You first and foremost. I ask that _____ would soak up the wisdom YOU have for him/her and not substitute it with the world's beliefs. I pray his/her leaf would not shrivel when hard circumstances come his/her way but that he/she would remain firm and strong in Your promises. God, I pray You would use _____'s sorrow to make him/her a stronger man, woman, boy, and girl for Your glory. Finally, I pray that _____'s gifts and goals would be prosperous—not for his/her personal pride, but to praise the One who blesses him/her and sees him/her through.*

I knew this passage. Or at least, I thought I did. It's amazing how Scripture comes **alive** each time you read it. Today, I want you to allow time to read this Psalm. Use it as a prayer. Delight and meditate over it. Rick Warren says, "The ultimate purpose of the Bible is not to inform us, it is to transform us." [2] Let's take **time** to **sit** by the water. Let's grow our roots deep and allow God's Word to transform our thinking. Most importantly, let's not stop praying, even at the ripe ole' age of 86, when it's dark and the lights have been turned out. Trees never grow too old to **pray.**

PRAYING the **PSALMS** is a great method of delighting and meditating on God's Word. Start with Psalm 1:1-3 and use this as a **PRAYER** to pray over someone that you love.

DAY TWO/ RESTING AT THE RIVER

I love how God can bring NEW meaning to Scripture each time we read it. Hebrews 4:12 tells us that God's Word is living and active. It is sharp. It penetrates our souls, spirits, joints, and marrow. God's Word goes deeper than surface conversation. He is the Master Surgeon using His Word as a scalpel to lovingly expose the intentions of our hearts. We can read it one day and find new meaning the next simply because it speaks directly to our circumstances. I love this about Scripture. I also know from experience that we have a CHOICE. Yes, God's Word is alive, but we have to ALLOW Him access. God will never force His way into our hearts.

- We have to CHOOSE to allow God's Word to penetrate our spirit and soak into our soul.

- We have to CHOOSE to allow God's Word to speak new meaning into our attitudes and circumstances.

- We have to CHOOSE to allow God's Word to be **PLANTED** into our hearts, so we will become the strong tree described in Psalm 1:3.

> "For the word of God is LIVING and ACTIVE. Sharper than any double-edged sword, it PENETRATES even to dividing soul and spirit, joints and marrow; it judges the thoughts and ATTITUDES of the heart."
>
> Hebrews 4:12

To allow growth takes—**TIME.** We are so busy rushing out the door and checking off our one-minute quiet times, we never seem to find time **to allow. PLANTED** is about deliberately choosing to sit by streams of water. We must let God's Word fill us, teach us, heal us, comfort us, and direct us through each day. Today, let's ALLOW some time and sit by the riverbank. (On a VERY cool note, Jeremiah 17:13 refers to the Lord Himself as the "spring of living water!") Grab your Bibles, take a seat with God, and let's take a closer look into the verses that surround Hebrews 4:12.

- **Read Hebrews 4:9-13.**
   (I like to read the verses slowly, sometimes more than once. If no one is home, I often read them out loud.)

> "Heaven and Earth were finished,
> down to the last detail.
> By the seventh day
> God had finished his work.
> On the seventh day
> he rested from all his work.
> God blessed the seventh day.
> He made it a Holy Day
> Because on that day
> he rested from his work,
> all the creating God had done."
>
> Genesis 2:1-3
> (MSG)

The one word that sums up the context of these verses is the _____ - rest for the people of God (verse 9).

The **Sabbath** was specifically created so God's children could have a day of rest— or perhaps busy moms could have an excuse not to do the dishes. I often wonder why God didn't create more than 24 hours in a day. I think He must have known how much we could jam pack into one 24-hour period! I am convinced God knew beforehand that man would try to **push** the boundary lines of time. Because of this, He designed specific days and hours so we would not exhaust ourselves from our "to-do" lists. He also knew we needed time to slow down and **REST.** Scripture also reminds us that the Sabbath, the seventh day, was established to be made holy and set apart.

- **Read the description of the seventh day in Genesis 2:1-3.**
- **As you delight and meditate on these verses, what specific things did God do on this day?**

_____

_____

The Message says that God finished creating Heaven and Earth "down to the **last** detail" (Genesis 2:1). **Nothing** was left undone, and **everything** was created perfectly. God completed His work, blessed the day, made it holy, and **rested.** Interestingly, the word for rested is *shabath,* meaning to keep as a day of rest. The idea appears to be that of **sitting down** or **sitting still.** It is also where we get the word **Sabbath.**

• What do the following verses say about God's PEACE and REST?
What is our part in these passages, and how can they change our attitudes?

• **Philippians 4:6-7** _____

_____

• **Psalm 29:11** _____

_____

• **Matthew 11:28** _____

_____

There is BLESSING in RESTING at the river. RESTING at the river means taking the time to SIT DOWN with God, pray, and cast our cares and concerns before Him (1 Peter 5:7). In return, He gives us STRENGTH and blesses us with PEACE. I don't know about you, but I want to run to this place of rest. I want to lay down my "to-do" list and replace it with the peace of Christ that will guard my mind and my heart.

• **What is on your heart today that you need to bring to God?** _____

_____

Let's take a look at John 1:1-4 that bridges Genesis 2:1-3 with Hebrews 4:9-13.

Read John 1:1-4. Please fill in the blanks. (I used the NIV translation.)
"*In the _____ was the Word, and the Word was _____ God, and the Word_____ God. _____was with God in the beginning. Through Him _____things were made; and without Him _____ was made that has been made. In Him was LIFE and that life was the _____of men.*"

• **Who was with God? Who was the Word?**

If you answered Jesus, you are correct! Here is the Scriptural proof that Jesus is God and was with God from the beginning. Since God's Word is alive and active (Hebrews 4:12), and Jesus is the WORD (John 1:1), then we also have proof that Jesus Himself is alive and active in our lives when we believe in Him. I can just imagine the creation of Heaven and Earth until NOTHING was left undone—no detail was left uncovered. They, the Father, Son, and Holy Spirit looked at each other and said, "It's time to BLESS and REST this day!"

Sometimes we get the idea we don't have time for God, and we are out the door before we can brush our teeth. But if we rush into our day without spending time with God, the more we are going to live on stress and fumes. When we are **PLANTED** and come with purpose to the river each day, we will discover that our whole day is more RESTFUL and PEACEFUL. While it is extremely important to keep the Sabbath holy, we do not have to wait for the seventh day to enjoy God's rest.

It is available everyday.

God says to make every effort to enter this rest. The word for rest in the Hebrews 4:9–13 passage is "*sabbatismos*"—a keeping of the Sabbath, the blessed rest from the toils and troubles in life. [3] Don't you want to cast your toils and troubles away? Come to the river where you will find REST. **Jesus is waiting.**

> "COME to ME, ALL you who are weary and burdened, and I WILL give you REST."
>
> Matthew 11:28

This week we are building the foundation for **PLANTED.** Today, I want you to grasp **THREE** foundational truths.

> **One:** God's WORD is alive and active.
> **Two:** God's WORD is a BLESSING over us where we can find REST when we SIT with Him.
> **Three:** God's WORD is created to be our STRENGTH as we walk with Him.

Let's combine all the Scripture we have studied and say this prayer.

Lord, thank You that I am blessed today because I have taken the time to delight in You. I pray to be planted by the stream of Living Water as I meditate on Your Word and allow Jesus to become alive and active in my heart. I desire to find peace and rest today as I give my cares and concerns to You. Replace my worry with Your peace that surpasses understanding and give me rest. If the storms of life blow through me today, I pray to remain strong and persevere because my roots are deep into Your Word of Truth. Amen.

DAY THREE/ WINDOW SHOPPING

Today we are going to sit by the river and grow our roots a little deeper. Let's go back to Psalm 1:1 and look into the description of this man. Okay, from now on, let's think of this person in our vernacular, as a woman. The "She" Tree (I just made myself laugh as I typed that!), is clearly too busy for God. She does not spend enough time with Him to allow the blessings in her life that He has to offer. Take note of her bodily position as we read these verses together.

"Blessed is the man who does not
> *__walk__ in the counsel of the wicked*
>> *or __stand__ in the way of sinners*
>>> *or __sit__ in the seat of mockers." Psalm 1:1*

> "How well God must like you— you don't hang out at **Sin Saloon,** you don't slink along ***Dead-End Road,*** you don't go to **Smart-Mouth College."**
>
> Psalm 1:1 (MSG)

It becomes clear that this man is **walking** in the counsel of the wicked, **standing** in the way of sinners, and **sitting** in the seat of mockers. I love how *The Message* expresses this truth. I bet we have all enrolled in "Smart-Mouth College" a time or two. In fact, I think I have spent more money there than I would like to admit.

This type of hanging and slinking and enrolling is almost like WINDOW SHOPPING. Have you ever casually walked by a store when something in the window caught your eye? It's not something you necessarily **need,** but when you stand there long enough (or short enough), you begin to rationalize that what you see is what you **want.** And when you take the first step forward, you might, just maybe, sit down in your decision to buy that particular item.

Walk. Stand. Sit.

I'm not saying window shopping is a **bad** thing. Although, if you are shopping at Anthropologie, you could be in BIG trouble. I know, it's so tempting!

Let's take a look at the first window shopper extraordinaire. Her name is Eve, and we can find her story in Genesis.

> • **Read the account of Eve in Genesis 3:1-7.**

The Bible tells us that Eve was walking around in the Garden of Eden. To my creative point, let's just say she is **window shopping** when she sees something that catches her attention. She stops, stands, and strikes up a conversation with the serpent who happens to be Satan. Eve listens to the enemy long enough to convince herself that the fruit God forbade her to eat is good for food, pleasing to the eye, and desirable for gaining wisdom. She takes it, eats it, and offers it to her husband. At this point, she has **walked** into temptation and **stood** long enough to be persuaded by the enemy that she needed the one thing God told her she could not have. Eve finally **sits** down in disobedience when she takes a bite of the forbidden fruit.

Walk. Stand. Sit.

- **Are you window shopping in the store of no-returns today?**
What in your life might be keeping you from being blessed by God?

_____

_____

_____

I wish temptation came with huge **flashing signs** that said:

- "WARNING, Do Not Enter!"
- "Children, do not walk with friends that make poor choices out of peer pressure. They will lead you astray."
- "Husbands and wives, stay clear of standing long enough in tempting situations!"
- "Stop looking at that man, get out of that bar, turn off the computer, do not sign the contract."
- "Sisters, do not sit with women that gossip, complain, and compare!"

Unfortunately, the enemy is much more clever. His temptation signs are packaged with words like these:
Fun, Pleasure, Satisfying, Good, Desirable, and Pleasing to the Eye (Genesis 3:1-7).

Why does the enemy not warn us with flashing lights? Because it's Satan's job to distract us from the **only** thing that can truly satisfy and give us peace—God's love.

Satan convinced Eve that God wasn't good enough to provide all she needed. And, he has the same agenda for us. He will tell you God isn't good enough. He will tell you that you are not good enough, smart enough, or pretty enough. He will whisper in your ear that you are a failure because your children did this or that. He will remind you of past mistakes. He will try to convince you God doesn't care that you lost your husband, your job, or your dream. He's like that. He's a deceiver. Satan's desire is to distract you from the care, the compassion, and the concern of the Almighty. Period.

- **What are some of the ways the enemy tries to convince you that God is not enough?**

_____

_____

_____

Although you may not get warning signs from the tempter, you can count on getting **live billboards** from God.

- **How do the following verses warn us about the ways of the world? What should our response be?**

  - **Romans 12:2** _____

  Our Response _____

  _____

  - **John 15:19** _____

  Our Response _____

  _____

  - **James 1:16, 22-27** _____

  Our Response _____

  _____

"Don't copy the **BEHAVIOR** and customs of this world, but **LET** God **TRANSFORM** you into a **NEW** person by changing the way you **THINK**. Then you will learn to know God's will for you, which is good and pleasing and PERFECT."

Romans 12:2 (NLT)

13

• **Read 1 John 2:15-17 and Proverbs 1:10. Why does God not want us to be attached to this world?**

_____

_____

Jesus warns us in Scripture NOT to become friends with this world. James tells us not to be deceived, but to take action and DO what the Word tells us. John teaches us that we do not belong to the world, but that Christ has chosen us out of the world. Romans 12:2 alerts us not to conform to the patterns of this world, i.e. walking with the wicked, standing in the way of sinners, sitting in the seat of mockers—but to be **transformed** by the renewing of your mind. These passages support the familiar phrase: ***To be in the world, but not of the world.***

> "You will keep in PERFECT PEACE all who TRUST in you, all whose thoughts are FIXED on you! TRUST in the LORD always, for the Lord God is the ETERNAL Rock."
>
> Isaiah 26:3-4 (NLT)

HOW do we do this? How do we RENEW our minds when the world is yelling in our faces to be this or to wear that? Again, our encouragement comes from the Word of God that is alive and active. We are to be **filled** with the Truth and **focus** on God each and every day. To renew means renewal, renovation, a change for the better.[4] Have you ever desired to renovate your home? Today we have the opportunity to renovate our hearts! We have an invitation to be firmly **PLANTED**—an opportunity to focus on God, the Master Designer and Architect, in the midst of this crazy world.

• **How do the following passages give us encouragement and help us to stay focused on God when window shopping wants to get the best of us?**

• **Isaiah 26:3-4** _____

_____

• **Colossians 3:1-2** _____

_____

• **2 Thessalonians 3:3,5** _____

_____

Let's close today by delighting in another passage of Scripture that reminds us to be **PLANTED**.

> "But blessed are those who trust in the Lord
>   and have made the Lord their hope and confidence.
> They are like trees planted along a riverbank,
>   with roots that reach deep into the water.
> Such trees are not bothered by the heat
>   or worried by long months of drought.
> Their leaves stay green,
>   and they never stop producing fruit."
> *Jeremiah 17:7-8 (NLT)*

> "If you look at the world, you'll be DISTRESSED. If you look within, you'll be DEPRESSED. If you look at **GOD** you'll be at **REST.**"[5]
>
> Corrie Ten Boom

We have so much more to study about this SHE TREE. I can hardly wait! For now, we must remember to TRUST in the Lord and not let the distractions of this world get our attention. Read the above quote from Corrie Ten Boom. I think this sums up our last three days together. Come and rest at the riverbank where we can focus on God's Word. Come and be like this tree with roots that reach deep into the water. Come and be PLANTED.

DAY FOUR/ SIT, STAND, WALK

Last Mother's Day, my sweet husband, Curry, took our family of six to Fernandina Beach for the weekend. It could not have been any better! We walked the quaint streets of downtown, ate at great restaurants, and stayed in the Hampton Inn right by the water. As a surprise, Curry took all the kids to school on Monday and let me stay to prepare for a women's luncheon. I knew I only had a couple of hours, so I went to the common breakfast area and got down to business. I set up my Bible, study guides, loaded up with Hampton Inn coffee, and started delighting in the Word of God! A sweet woman came up to me and said, "It's so good to see you studying God's Word!" I asked her if she would pray for me. She agreed. She promised to go straight to her room and even invite her husband to get on his knees, too!

As God began to reveal His Word to me, I became more and more excited. My body language must have been showing this because another woman came up to me and said, "You are going to need to slow down! Your studying is too intense!" To my surprise she said, "My sister told me she was praying for you." At that, I looked at her with pleading eyes and said, "You need to tell your sister to STOP because I am not sure if I can take much more of what God is sharing with me!"

Today, I am grateful to be able to share with you what God revealed to me that day in the common breakfast room. Yesterday, we looked at two things: First, we took note of the **bodily position** of the man in Psalm 1:1. Second, we studied the ways of God that are different from the ways of the world.

> • **What does Isaiah 55:8 tell us about the ways of God?** _____
> _____

God's thoughts are not our thoughts, and God's ways are not like ours. I believe it is true to say that God is **counter-cultural** to the ways of this world. As believers in Christ, we are different from the person depicted in Psalm 1:1. Why? Because God's economy is the reverse of the world's. We do not walk in the counsel of the wicked, stand in the way of sinners, or sit in the seat of mockers. Rather, in God's economy, our actions are in the **reverse order.**

> **First, we have to SIT in the presence of God,**
> **to strengthen us to STAND on His promises,**
> **so that we may WALK in His purposes.**

Did you get that? Are you as excited as I am? Read it again slowly and maybe you won't fall out of your chair like I did. This is what **PLANTED** is all about.

We **SIT** in God's presence.
We **STAND** on His promises.
We **WALK** in His purposes. In that exact order: **sit, stand, walk.**

If we charge out of the door each morning walking into the world of deadlines, carpools, yoga classes, board rooms, classrooms, tennis courts, and grocery stores, we will find ourselves stumbling all over the place. We will say things we don't mean and do things we will regret later. Just as a baby doesn't walk coming out of the womb, (praise Jesus!) we **first** have to learn to sit. It starts at the RIVER.

As we begin the journey of **PLANTED**, my prayer is that we will discover what it means to **sit, stand, and walk** with Jesus. I pray we will recognize the warning signs when we start window shopping into temptation. Forfeiting the blessing was never God's intention for Eve, and it is never His intention for us. God intends for us … to be **PLANTED.**

• **What does James 1:21 tell us about being PLANTED in God's Word?**

_____

_____

James tells us to humbly accept the Word **PLANTED** in us because it can save us. Save us from what? **Planting** God's Word in our hearts will save us from walking in the way of the wicked, standing with sinners, and sitting in the seat of mockers. God's desire for us is to wake up each and every day, sit with Him, and discover the Living Word that soaks into and pierces our very souls. By this, we are FILLED to **stand** on His promises and **walk** in His purposes.

The truths about this tree are many. For now, I want this prayer to be a blessing over you.

> *Oh, Sweet Lord, I pray for all of us today to be strengthened and encouraged to live an empowered life that is only sustained by You, a Holy God. I pray we would find time to sit with You this week and discover Your Living Word that gives us the desire and power to do what pleases You. I pray we would not walk, stand, or sit in temptation, but instead sit in Your Word so we can stand on Your promises and walk in Your purposes. I pray that if life takes an unexpected turn, our leaf would not wither because we have drawn from Your stream this morning. May the fruit of our hands, mouth, and feet be sweet and full of service for You. I ask that whatever we do today would be prosperous, not for personal gain, but for the glory of the One who deserves all the praise. Amen.*

Fellow tree, let's not get it backwards today. Let's not go window shopping into the store of no returns. Instead, let's allow time to SIT by the **Stream of Living Water** where we can grow our roots deep, become stronger in anticipation for the storms of life, and keep our leaves from withering because **our hope is in the Lord.**

DAY FIVE/ PREPARATION

In my small group, a friend shared with me how she opens her prayers each morning. She asks *the Lord to prepare her for what He is preparing for her that day.* Read that again slowly. I connected her prayer with a song I heard on the radio by Cloverton:

> *"Take me into the beautiful where the river flows … "*

I know I'm in "tree-mode" when I start connecting prayers and songs with anything having to do with trees, rivers, or fruit! This day, God allowed me to connect my friend's prayer with this song. **Conclusion?** God is PREPARING us to come to **the beautiful** everyday. It is a place where the river **flows.** The word "flow" is most important because rivers that don't flow are disgusting. Algae, bacteria, and scum form in motionless waters. I remember the days of getting alcohol in my ears every time I would swim in a warm water lake in Florida. My husband's camp used to call the homemade concoction, "camel snot." The point is: **Stagnant lakes don't flow.** Neither do we when we make the choice not to spend time sitting with God. God's Word is made to be alive, not stagnant. A simple alcohol concoction will not be enough. We need God's Living Stream to be constantly flowing through us washing away the scum of our bacteria-ridden lives.

I was convicted one Sunday that people often go to church and politely dip their "big toe" in the river long enough to prove to themselves (or others) that they are good enough Christians. The problem is our toes dry off quickly, and we are back to the worldly routines that dehydrate our days. God wants to meet us at the river everyday where we allow His Word to flow through us. Checking off the "God box" on a Sunday morning will never be enough to satisfy our souls. As a result, our relationship with the LIVING God will become stagnant. This is not a beautiful place where the river flows.

"Take me into the
BEAUTIFUL
Won't you take me
back again
With a love
unexplainable
Come and FILL up this
dry land
Let it OPEN our eyes
To see a world we've
never seen
Let it open our
HEARTS up
To feel You INSIDE of
us
You're HERE inside of
me

Take me into the
BEAUTIFUL
Where the
RIVERS flow
Where the love that
NEVER ENDS …"[6]

Cloverton

I don't know about you, but I want to jump into the river! I want to go **deep** with God and get **sopping wet**. I want to tell people about my conversations at the river. Let me ask you a question. Have you ever met someone who radiated peace and joy? Have you ever asked them why? You might just find that their **true satisfaction** and **peace** comes from getting soaking wet with the life that only Jesus offers. I came to this realization the same year Steven Curtis Chapman's song, *DIVE* was released. I wonder if he overheard my thoughts. Perhaps God convicted him of the same thing. The lyrics are printed below:

"I'm diving in, I'm going DEEP, in over my head, I want to be,
Caught in the rush, lost in the flow, in over my head, I want to go
The river's deep, the RIVER'S wide, the river's water is ALIVE
So sink or swim, I'M DIVING IN

There is a supernatural power
In this mighty river's flow
It can bring the dead to life
And it can fill an empty soul
And give a heart the only thing
Worth living and worth dying for yeah
But we will never know the awesome POWER
Of the GRACE of GOD
Until we let ourselves get swept away
Into this holy flood
So if you'll take my hand
We'll close our eyes and count to three
And take the leap of faith
Come on let's go"[7]

Let's get **PLANTED** and go DEEP with God. Don't just feel the water swoosh around your toes on Sunday morning, but let the Holy water swirl around the roots of your faith everyday.

God is the main water line, and through belief in His Son, we are allowed **access** to worship Him, anytime, **anywhere.**

Coming to the "beautiful" where the river flows (where God prepares our hearts for the day) can look different for all of us. A good friend of mine shared with me that her "beautiful," or let's just call it the riverbank, was her kitchen sink. She had small children at the time and always found herself at the sink washing—something. The basin filled with water became her mini-sanctuary where she would pray over her girls and thank God for all of her blessings.

We all have different places of "beautiful" that flow from the main source of the Living God to irrigate our souls. For some, it could be the break of dawn before anyone wakes up. It could be the quiet drive to pick **up** the kids. It could be a walk at night when the sun has gone down, the golf course (my husband's favorite sanctuary), or even the kitchen sink.

If I had my ideal riverbank, it would be on our side porch in cool weather with a nice hot cup of coffee. A candle would be lit and quietness would surround me except for the birds that gather at our bird feeder. That's the ideal. But in Florida, it is usually buggy, muggy, and hot. There goes my sanctuary. I will settle for the little brown couch in my office … with air conditioning.

There is no perfect formula for **where** you go to find your quiet river spot—the important part is that you **GO.**

- **Where is your "riverbank" where you sit with God?**
Where do you prepare your heart to dive deep into His Word?

_____
_____
_____
_____
_____
_____

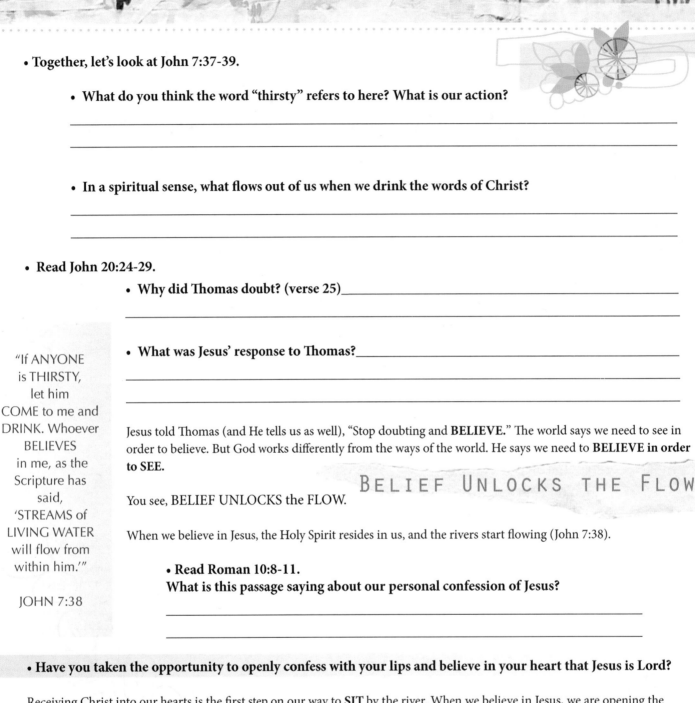

- **Together, let's look at John 7:37-39.**

    - **What do you think the word "thirsty" refers to here? What is our action?**

    _____

    _____

    - **In a spiritual sense, what flows out of us when we drink the words of Christ?**

    _____

    _____

- **Read John 20:24-29.**

        - **Why did Thomas doubt? (verse 25)** _____

    _____

        - **What was Jesus' response to Thomas?** _____

    _____

    _____

> "If ANYONE is THIRSTY, let him COME to me and DRINK. Whoever BELIEVES in me, as the Scripture has said, 'STREAMS of LIVING WATER will flow from within him.'"
>
> JOHN 7:38

Jesus told Thomas (and He tells us as well), "Stop doubting and **BELIEVE.**" The world says we need to see in order to believe. But God works differently from the ways of the world. He says we need to **BELIEVE in order to SEE.**

BELIEF UNLOCKS THE FLOW

You see, BELIEF UNLOCKS the FLOW.

When we believe in Jesus, the Holy Spirit resides in us, and the rivers start flowing (John 7:38).

- **Read Roman 10:8-11.**
  What is this passage saying about our personal confession of Jesus?

  _____

  _____

- **Have you taken the opportunity to openly confess with your lips and believe in your heart that Jesus is Lord?**

Receiving Christ into our hearts is the first step on our way to **SIT** by the river. When we believe in Jesus, we are opening the floodgates and allowing Christ's love to flow through us, counsel over us, convict us, and walk us through life. Ephesians 3:12 says, "_In Christ, we can come before God with freedom and confidence and without fear. We can do this through faith in Christ_" (NCV). The river becomes our access any day or night to be with our Lord and to grow up into the strong tree that will persevere through the toughest of storms and in the happiest of days.

Are we being prepared for what God is preparing us for?
Are we meeting with Him _"at the beautiful"_ where the river flows?
Are we diving in to the awesome power and grace of God?

This is just the beginning of **PLANTED.**
Are you ready to get wet?
Throw out the camel snot, I'm diving in!

EXTRA VERSES BY THE STREAM:

To explore more about the foundation of Christianity and the need for confession in Christ, please read:

- **Romans 3:23** … Who has sinned and falls short of God's glory?
- **Romans 5:8** … How did God demonstrate His love for us?
- **Romans 6:23** … Why did God have to die?
- **Romans 8:1-2** … How are we free in Christ?
- **Romans 10:13** … Who will be saved?

VIEWER GUIDE: SESSION ONE
THERE IS BLESSING IN THE RESTING

"May the Lord DIRECT your HEARTS into God's LOVE and CHRIST'S perseverance."

2 Thessalonians 3:5

I have been praying for you this week! I pray you are beginning to grasp the concept of being a tree PLANTED by streams of water where we Sit, Stand, and Walk with Jesus. When we meditate and delight on God's Word, we will be prosperous in all we do!

1. Romans 12:1 reminds us not to be conformed to the patterns of this world, but to RENEW our minds. Renew means: _____. God is the perfect Interior Decorator. He is renovating our hearts.

2. We need to _____ by the river. Every time we make **the choice** to come and rest by the river, we will be BLESSED. When we give God our worries, our heartache, our concerns, and our troubles, He replaces them with His strength.

* **May the Lord direct your hearts …**

3. 2 Thessalonians 3:5 says: "May the Lord _____ your HEARTS into God's _____ and CHRIST'S perseverance." When we guard our heart first, streams of Living Water will flow from it. When we plant ourselves in the ways of the world, we will only find an artificial, temporary satisfaction. When we plant ourselves by the stream of Living Water we will be _____.

* May the Lord direct your hearts into **God's Love and Christ's perseverance.**

4. We have the same power of Christ's perseverance in our simple decision making. When God directs our hearts into His love and Christ's perseverance, we receive His power.

5. Satan posed as something _____. The great deceiver clothed himself as a serpent, one of God's good creatures (NIV notes on Genesis 3:1). It is the battle of good and evil. When we stand long enough to believe the deception, we fall into sin. Jesus came to "break the spell" of sin and free us forever.

6. What in your life looks GOOD but might be evil in disguise? We need to filter our decisions through the TRUTH of God's Word.

7. James 1:5-6 says, "If any of you lacks _____, you should ask God, who gives GENEROUSLY without finding fault, and it will be given to you. But when you ask, you must _____ and not _____, because the one who doubts in like a wave of the sea, blown and tossed by the wind."

• Stop _____ and BELIEVE. **BELIEF unlocks the FLOW.**

> *"For everything that trips you up, we must replace with a TRUTH from God.*
> *When I am satisfied with God and filled up with His truth, I can stop having the unrealistic*
> *expectations from people, possessions, and positions."* ~ **Lysa TerKeurst**

8. **Unrealistic expectations.** Believing what the world says over what God's TRUTH says will always give us a false message. God's truth unlocks the flow of Christ within us, and we look different. Our beauty comes from the Lord, not from the world.

Galatians 5:1
"It is for freedom that Christ has set us free. Stand_____, then, and do not let yourselves be
burdened again by a yoke of slavery."

9. God is alive and working in _____ giving us power and desire to please Him (Philippians 2:13).

10. **Closing Points:** Rest at the river. Do not conform to the patterns of this world. Renovate your heart. Let the Lord direct His love over you. Replace your doubts with the truth. Believe and do not doubt. Believe in order to SEE. Release the power of the Holy Spirit. Find your "beautiful" by the stream of Living Water.

NOTES:

WEEK TWO: Day One/ THE INVITATION
TO SIT CRISS-CROSS, APPLESAUCE ~
LIKE A CHILD

I was studying for **PLANTED** one morning when my seven-year old began vying for my attention. He was wiggling around and, quite frankly, I was getting a bit irritated. "John-John, this is Mommy's quiet time," I humphed. After all, it was EARLY on a Saturday morning.

To "humph" means:

> interjection, a snort, articulated with a voiceless onset and ending in a nasal stop.[1]

John-John was persistent. He inched his way closer and closer, until I realized that all he wanted to do was sit in my lap. Ding-dong—anyone home?

I am ashamed to tell you that I was studying about the children wanting to **SIT** in Jesus' lap. I was struck by the analogy. Jesus wants us to come and to SIT in His lap, too. He is never too busy. Never distracted. Never studying too hard. And Jesus has probably never "humphed" before.

On the contrary, **Jesus invites.**

> • **Let's read the story in Mark 10:13-16.**
>
> > • **Why were the people bringing their children to Jesus?**
> > _____
> > _____
> > _____
>
> > • **Why do you believe the touch from Jesus was so important to them?**
> > _____
> > _____
> > _____
>
> > • **What were the attitudes of the disciples and Jesus' response?**
> > _____
> > _____
> > _____
>
> > • **What physical action did Jesus take that demonstrated His love?**
> > _____
> > _____
> > _____

> "One day some parents brought their children to Jesus so he could **TOUCH** and **BLESS** them. But the disciples scolded the parents for bothering him. When Jesus saw what was happening, he was angry with his disciples. He said to them, 'Let the children COME to me. Don't stop them! For the Kingdom of God belongs to those who are like these children.'"
>
> Mark 10:13-14 (NLT)

I am sad to say my attitude with John-John was more like the disciples. But Jesus' attitude is one of love and compassion. He had all the time in the world to bless these little ones. What a great lesson for us. Jesus invites us to come and **SIT like a child.**

Psalm 1:1-3 describes two different people: One that is blessed and one that is not. I personally think we can move in and out of these two characters. I am the first to tell you there have been many days when I did not receive a blessing because I was sitting around in my sinful self, trying to steer my own stroller. I think it is important to note that while our belief in Jesus saves us from our sin and makes us right before God, we are still sinful creatures (1 John 1:7-9). We still have the capacity to sin and make bad choices. This is the very reason why we need to be **PLANTED** each day.

> • **How did Paul describe himself in Romans 7:15-25?**
> (Warning: Read this slowly, you might be prone to humph.)
>
> _____
>
> _____
>
> • **What was his specific struggle?**
>
> _____
>
> _____
>
> • **In what ways can you relate to this idea of wanting and trying to do good, but at same time seeming to fall short?**
>
> _____
>
> _____

I'll never forget the day I took our SUV to be detailed. I was a bit skeptical because I KNEW the dealership could never resurrect our family truckster back to the **first** day of sanitized ownership— especially since four children had been blessing it. To say that I was **under**whelmed with the results would be an **under**statement. "There is **still** gum on the seat belt, almonds smashed between the console, and crumbs on my driver's seat," I said. The vehicle inspection lady looked at me, twitched, and reported, "This is the WORST SUV I have ever seen. It has already been back to the detail shop **three** times for cleaning!" I was horrified. She obviously had not sat in Jesus' lap that morning.

I will never be able to keep my car in mint condition while living the carpooling, snack-eating, sports-equipment storing, back-packing life we live. It's like trying to brush your teeth while eating an Oreo cookie. Although this might be a gross analogy, it illustrates that as much as I want to and **try** to keep my car clean, I will always fall short. In the same way, as much as I want to and **try** to keep my life free from sin (i.e., holding back snappy comments from inspection ladies, wandering worry, or humphing), I will always fall short. That's why I need to sit on Jesus' lap every day. How about you?

> "'I tell you the TRUTH, anyone who doesn't receive the Kingdom of God like a CHILD will never enter it.' Then he took the children in his arms and placed his HANDS on their heads and **BLESSED** them."
>
> Mark 10:15-16 (NLT)

EXTRA TIME BY THE STREAM:

Meditate on Mark 10:13-16. Ask yourself these personal questions:

- • **Why do YOU come to Jesus?**

- • **Why do YOU yearn for His touch?**

- •**What is YOUR attitude when someone needs the touch of Jesus through you?**

- • **What physical action do you take to show Jesus' love?**

Day TWO/ The Invitation to Rest

- **Let's begin by reading Matthew 11:28-30.**

  - **Who is Jesus inviting to come? If we go, what will we find? What is Christ offering us?**

  _____

  _____

There are two meanings for the word **rest** in this passage. In verse 28, rest is *anapauo* meaning "to offer rest."[2] The second word *anapausis*, found in verse 29, means "inward tranquility while one performs necessary labor."[3] When I consider how to sit, delight, and meditate on God's Word, I envision climbing into the lap of God, receiving not only a blessing, but also rest. Jesus is **not** the scary Santa Claus in the mall who listens to our wants for Christmas. He is our friend. He is humble, gentle in heart, and He is **inviting** us to come. He identifies with the fact that we are weary, overworked, and sometimes stressed-out. He knows that, just like Paul, we are trying to be good. He knows we are trying to do the right thing, but often mess up. I love the fact that the two words for rest both start with "ana" meaning again. **Again and again**, we can come. **Again and again**, the invitation is open. **Again and again,** we can come as broken vessels. We don't have to RSVP or check the accept box on our E vite. He invites us to learn from Him and to learn about Him. His yoke is easy, and His burden is light. A yoke was used on an ox, a strong domestic animal, utilized to carry the weight of work to be done. Jesus wants to carry the weight of our burdens too. He is more than delighted to listen to our problems, our fears, our worries, and even what we want for Christmas.

- **What do you need to tell Jesus today as you sit with Him?**

  _____

  _____

- **Read 1 Peter 5:6-7.**
- **What should our attitude be like when we come into the presence of God?**

  _____

  _____

- **What is God asking you to do today? Why?**

  _____

  _____

"HUMBLE yourselves, therefore, under God's MIGHTY hand, that he may LIFT YOU UP in due time. CAST all your anxiety on him because HE cares for YOU."

1 Peter 5:6-7

My husband and I try to go on a date-night once a week. It's a great time to catch up and remind ourselves that at one point in our lives, we had no kids, no carpools, and no Saturday morning games. My mentor tells me that we should never stop dating our husbands. I agree. Date-nights are filled with adult conversations and a reminder that we still love each other. What I love about these date nights is that, sometimes, I will get what I call a "**golden nugget**"—a piece of really good information we have not had time to discuss during the week. Today, I have a golden nugget for you. **CAST.**

I have always understood that "to cast" was to throw with all your might … taking your burdens and throwing them as far as you could. My pastor shared with me a deeper "golden nugget." To cast means to throw **upon**, to cast **upon**, to give up to God. Using this analogy, we are not just casting our cares into thin air, but **UPON** the foot of the cross where our sins are forgiven once and for all. How cool is that?

I want to point out a word that connects Matthew 11:28-30 and 1 Peter 5:5-7. The word is **humility.** Our attitude should be one of humility when we come to Jesus. Humility means:

to destroy the power of, the independence of, not arrogant or prideful, marked by meekness, modesty in behavior, attitude or spirit.[4]

The Greek word for humble is *tapeinos* and gives us an even deeper meaning. It means:

not rising far from the ground, devoid of all haughtiness.[5]

Do you see the tree imagery here? Trees do not grow independent from the nutrients of the soil in which they are PLANTED. A tree can't grow up until it **grows down.** Likewise, we cannot grow UP in our faith until our roots are deep into the rich soil of God's Word. **Humble.**

A TREE CAN'T GROW UP UNTIL IT GROWS DOWN

In Matthew 11:30, Jesus describes Himself as being gentle and **humble** in heart. It is the same Greek word. Jesus will never ask something from us that He Himself has not experienced.

- **Read Hebrews 4:15-16.**

  - **As you delight on these verses, what words personally speak to you?**

  _____

  _____

  _____

Because of Jesus' life, death, and resurrection, our belief in Him gives us **access** to come to the throne of grace with confidence. *The Message* says:

"We don't have a priest who is out of touch with our reality. He's been through weakness and testing, experienced it all—all but the sin. So let's walk right up to Him and get what He is so ready to give. Take the mercy, accept the help." Hebrews 4:15-16

Jesus is **reachable** and **approachable.** He can relate to everything we experience. He sympathizes with our weaknesses without judgment. Jesus is **humble.**

The people that brought their children to Jesus knew something we need to know. Jesus is approachable. Spend time with Him because He cares for you. Sit on His lap and find rest. There is no limit to how long you can sit or how many times you go. He is always there, always waiting. Most importantly, don't get up until He puts His hand on your head and blesses you. Mark 10:16 specifically tells us that Jesus took the children in His arms, put His hands on them, and blessed them. In her book, *More than a Good Bible Study Girl*, Lysa TerKeurst shares that she does not get up from her quiet times until she feels the blessing of God.

"I don't stop spending time with the Lord until I've learned something or received something from Him; therefore, every moment spent with the Lord is time well spent."[6]

Good point. Don't get up until you feel the rest that is offered, even in the turmoil, and sense that all is well with your soul. Can you hear the ancient hymn? Let's sing it together. By the river.

IT IS WELL WITH MY SOUL

"When peace, like a river, attendeth my way,
When sorrows like sea billows roll;
Whatever my lot, Thou has taught me to say,
It is well, it is well, with my soul.
Refrain: It is well, with my soul,
It is well, it is well, with my soul." [7]

DAY THREE/ THE INVITATION TO BELIEVE

Ever since I was a little girl, I have always wanted to be older. I guess you can blame this on the fact that I was the youngest of four girls. I wanted to dress, look, and act like my older sisters. When they would leave for college, I would give them a wave goodbye and dash into their rooms to see what I could pilfer.

Today, magazines, TV, the internet, Facebook, and lyrics in popular music are shouting at our children that they need to grow up—way too fast. This worldly noise gets pretty loud in my head, too. When my children were little, God gave me a picture that my life was similar to being on a conveyor belt, just rolling along with "The Joneses." God forbid someone to act out of the ordinary and get off the belt, like signing up your child with a different ballet studio! You can almost hear the conveyor belt come to a screeching stop, while everyone stares at you. It reminds me of inspector woman.

Jesus reminds us once again that **His ways are different** from the ways of this world. His thoughts are higher than ours, too. Thank goodness!

• **Let's read Matthew 18:1-4 and answer the following questions.**

> "Therefore, whoever HUMBLES himself like this child is the GREATEST in the kingdom of heaven."
>
> Matthew 18:4

• **What is the topic of conversation between the disciples and Jesus?**

_____

_____

• **Who did Jesus use to visually convey His response?**

_____

_____

• **What do you think it means to change and become like little children? Think about the playfulness, innocence, and trust of a child.**

_____

_____

• **Can you do that?**

• **What word do you recognize again that we studied yesterday?** _____

Humility. We see it again. God has a reason for repeating Himself in Scripture. I need the repetition. How about you?

> "Therefore, whoever humbles himself like this child is greatest in the kingdom of heaven." Matthew 18:4

An oxymoron, right? **Humility** and **greatest** are usually not two words that work together. But in kingdom language, they do.

• **What do the following verses tell us about humility and greatness?**

• **Romans 12:10-13**

_____

_____

_____

- **Philippians 2:1-5**

_____

_____

- **Mark 10:43-45**

_____

_____

Honor one another before yourself. In humility, consider others better than yourself. The first shall be last and the last shall be first. Humble yourselves like children, you will be **great** in the kingdom of Heaven. What does it take to enter the kingdom of Heaven? We talked about this last week. It takes a belief in Jesus Christ. Why would God make the analogy that we should change to become like children? It's simple. **Children believe.** Instead of "What would Jesus do?" bracelets, I think we need to make "What would the children do" bracelets. They believe. Good grief—we can get them to believe anything from the Easter Bunny to tiny elves that sit on our shelves and report to Santa whether we are good or bad. But there is a **distinction.** Jesus boldly begins this passage with words that separate fairy tales from reality:

I TELL YOU THE TRUTH.

Boom. Jesus' words have **power.** We have studied this from day one. His words are alive and active and sharper than a two-edged sword. Swords are used in battle. When it comes to the children of God, you better believe that Jesus is fighting for you.

> "The LORD will FIGHT for YOU; you need ONLY to be STILL."
>
> Exodus 14:14

- **What does Exodus 14:14 say about fighting?**

_____

_____

- **What is God doing, and what is our position?**

_____

_____

Being still is the one thing little children don't do very well. Neither do we. Maybe that's why they had to physically get on His lap. I know if I actually got to sit on Jesus' lap, I would be all eyes and ears. Today, the physical is impossible. Jesus has risen and sits at the right hand of God. But Scripture reminds us that nothing is impossible for God (Matthew 19:26). We are invited to come and SIT. Whether you imagine yourself plopped right into His lap like a child or sitting beside the stream having tea, the idea is that you are SITTING at His invitation. When we sit, we learn, we rest, and we are blessed. **Amazing.**

DAY FOUR/ THE INVITATION
TO BE FILLED TO OVERFLOWING

- Let's take a quick look at Matthew 11:25, just three verses above where Jesus invites us to come.

  - **To whom is God revealing the hidden things? What is He revealing to them?**

_____

_____

Let's take this verse in two parts. We will study one part today—then examine the second part tomorrow. **First,** to whom is God revealing the hidden things? (Again we see repetition is good.) It is God's pleasure to reveal these things to the **little children**. Why not reveal the truth to people who are wise and learned, to those who **think** they are smart? *The Message* refers to them as the "sophisticates and know-it-alls." Again, **children believe.**

Children are naturally honest and tell you what they think. They have not built up walls of insecurity or worldly philosophy. They have no airs about them. They are vulnerable, and they unconditionally love and trust. They are not proud, but rather, they are humble and gentle. I also know that children don't have a measuring cup to gauge the size of God. Look at what we read in children's books about love: I love you to the moon and back.[8] I love you to here and beyond. There is no measure. There is no measure for God's love either. His love is limitless. **His love is immeasurable.**

> • **Read Ephesians 3:14-19.**
> (This Ephesians passage is one we will come back to often, but for now, I want to focus on verse 19.)
>
> > • **What is Paul's prayer in verse 19?**
> >
> > _____
> >
> > _____

Paul is praying for the whole body of Christ to know that God's love surpasses man's knowledge. This drives "the wise" and "know-it-alls" crazy. Why? They are more comfortable putting God in a box where they can be in charge and make the calls. Control fills them. Control satisfies them. In this verse, Paul is praying that we would not be filled with "knowledge," but that we would be filled to the measure of **ALL** the fullness of God. How can this be?

Does anyone remember the old **BRIM** coffee commercials? "Fill it to the rim with Brim." I like to say, "Fill it to the rim with HIM!" To be filled to the measure of God is something we cannot … measure. God is God, and we are not (another great Steven Curtis Chapman song). We cannot measure God, but boy, do we try! Instead of seeing him immeasurable and putting our complete trust in Him, **we resist Him.**

> • **Have you ever tried to put a measure on God or put a limit on what He can do in your life?**
>
> _____
>
> _____

> • **When is it hardest to completely trust that God loves you and has a plan that is good for your life?**
>
> _____
>
> _____

> • **What do these verses say about trusting in the unlimited capability of God?**
>
> > • **Ephesians 3:20-21**
> >
> > _____
> >
> > _____
> >
> > • **Jeremiah 29:11-14**
> >
> > _____
> >
> > _____

God is immeasurable, and His power can work in us far beyond what we could expect or even imagine. He also has a plan for us that is good. He invites us to call upon Him, to come to Him, and to pray to Him.

Although **we** may put a limit on God's capabilities, it is interesting to note that **nature does not resist God.** Trees don't resist God. Children don't resist God. I want to add that there is a BIG difference between being childish and childlike. The childish are the "know-it-alls" who force God to fit into their rules rather than accepting the TRUTH that sets them free from the weariness. Good grief, they are still arguing about who's going to be the greatest in Heaven (Luke 22:24). But what about the childlike? They represent the tree in Psalm one. They are having a blast reaching their limbs up in praise, sitting with Jesus by the riverbank, finding Him immeasurable, and being **blessed!**

Do you see the difference?

Two summers ago, we stayed in Grand Junction, Colorado. We were walking downtown when my kids spotted JUMPING water fountains. All they could say was, "Can we, Mom? Can we?" We had just eaten dinner, and we were headed back to our hotel. "Oh, why not? Have fun!" I said as they jumped in … fully clothed. For the next thirty minutes, Curry and I got to watch our kids have the time of their lives getting completely soaked. We were **all** blessed that night. I, like the parents who brought their kids to Jesus, loved seeing them **feel the joy** as they were **touched** by the water. No sophistication here.

I'll close today with this TREE imagery.

> "I spread my HANDS out to YOU,
> My soul THIRSTS for you like a parched land."
> Psalm 143:6

Can't you see this tree dancing in the jumping water fountains? This tree is spreading out her branches high and glorious. Her roots are digging deep in the rich soil of God to receive the restful, prayerful, delightful surge of cool refreshing water. The source feeds the soul, and we are **satisfied.**

Oh Lord, fill me today with the fullness of You so that I am filled to overflowing! I pray I would be reminded that You have no limit to Your love. I pray to sit with You each day so You can wash my worries away. Fill me with rest and the spirit of a child so that I may dance in Your fountain. I need Your spiritual water so I may overflow to spill Your love and goodness on others. Teach me Lord, to put others before myself and to come to You with the faith of a child. Lord, I pray to sit until I receive the blessing. Thank You Jesus, that I can come again and again. I spread my arms out to You in praise. My soul thirsts for You. Fill me to stand on Your promises that I have learned this week. Fill me so that I may walk in Your purposes. Praise You, O Lord.
Amen.

"And I ask him that with both feet PLANTED firmly on LOVE, you'll be able to take in with all followers of Jesus the EXTRAVAGANT dimensions of Christ's LOVE. Reach out and experience the breadth! Test its length! Plumb the depths! Rise to the heights! Live full lives, full in the FULLNESS of God."

EPHESIANS 3:18-19
(MSG)

Day Five/ The Invitation
to the Things of God

Today, let's focus on the second part of Matthew 11:25.

God is revealing these things to the little children. What are these **things**? Let me interject—I love that God uses the word, "things" in this passage. I do it all the time! For example when I ask my daughter, "Daley, would you please get me that **thing** over there." She knows exactly what I mean.

A couple of Christmases ago, I bought my seven-year-old daughter a wooden ironing board and a plastic iron. Upon opening them, she squealed with delight, "Mommy, I got a **thing** to go with my **thing**!" I realize that I am exposing you to the fact I do not iron enough for my child to identify these household appliances. The point is… I knew exactly what she meant. Why? Because I **know** my daughter.

The more we get to **know** God and the "things" of God, we will discover the hidden mysteries of Scripture. The things God is referring to in Matthew 11 are the **TRUTHS of God.**

- **Let's read Luke 12:22-34.**

    - **What is Jesus telling His disciples NOT to do?**

    _____

    _____

    - **What is the first action we should take when sitting by the river?**

    _____

    _____

    - **What are the promises from this passage on which we can stand today?**

    _____

    _____

    - **How does Jesus refer to the disciples in verse 32?**

    _____

    _____

Jesus is reminding us again that we have an open invitation to come to Him—like a child. He tells us not to worry. He tells us to seek Him first … before our minds get clogged with the worries of today. Can I make a suggestion? When you come, turn off your computer, your phone, your I-pad, your "to-do" list, and your agenda for the day. I believe the reason we worry so much is that there is **too much** to keep track of! How many texts, e-mails, Instagram, and Facebook messages can we possibly get in one day? Our time by the river is **sacred**. Focus on Him **first**. Let's be still and **seek** the Truths of God.

"Seek ye first the kingdom of God and all these things shall be added unto you." Luke 12:31

The Hebrew word for **seek** is: "darash" meaning: to inquire, search, seek with care, frequent a place, consult, investigate, ask for practice, meditate, study, follow, seek with applications [9]

- **Circle the word that speaks to you as you sit with the Lord and seek Him first.**

I would love to see the ones you circled! Did you find the word that is used in the first Psalm? **Meditate.** Yes! Seeking is delighting and meditating on God's Word.

- **What do the following verses say about seeking the Lord. What is promised?**

    - **Psalm 105:4**

    _____

    _____

    - **Jeremiah 29:13**

    _____

    _____

    - **Jeremiah 10:21**

    _____

    _____

Let's not be senseless and start our day without the Lord. In Jeremiah 10:21, _The Message_ substitutes the word senseless with stupid. I don't know about you, but I do not want to be stupid.

Definition of **stupid**: a low SAT score when someone misses a row on the "bubble-in" sheet. I will never forget the day I ran to the mailbox with high aspirations of college when … I opened the envelope. My heart sank. I felt like I was the most stupid student on earth. Dumb as they get. Why was I in AP English when I couldn't even score a high grade on the Scholastic Aptitude Test (I did have to spell check aptitude!) After all—I was smart, wasn't I?

Seek the Lord and find His strength. Seek the Lord with all your heart, and He will be found by you. Seek the Lord and fix your eyes on Him, not the world. Be transformed by the renewing of your mind. SIT with Him, and do not get up until you sense the blessing. Rest in Him. Cast your cares on Him, and He will give you peace. Give thanks in all things … even bad SAT scores. Whew. I feel much better. And smarter.

Things are the treasures of Truth found in Scripture, the promises of God on which we stand. The more we come to the river to delight and meditate on His Word, the better acquainted we are with the things of God. The more we seek Him, the more blessings we will receive.

While it is true I will never win a star in Heaven for having the cleanest SUV, the highest SAT score, or the fact my daughter does not know what an iron is, I can always come to Jesus like a child, SIT on His lap, and give Him my weariness. I believe my God calls me blessed simply because **I come.** Blessed means: "to praise, to celebrate with praises, to ask God's blessing on a thing" (funny, even the Merriam-Webster dictionary uses the word, _things_).[10] I pray TODAY we can all feel this blessing as we come. **The invitation is open.**

> _Lord, thank You for another week of study. You offer me a gracious invitation to come. I don't have to get dressed up_
> _or put on airs. I am invited to come as I am. Because of the sacrifice Jesus made for me, I can come with freedom_
> _and confidence. Jesus is reachable and accessible. He is in touch with my reality, and I can cast my cares upon Him._
> _Don't let me waste another day without spending time with You. Fill me to overflowing, and help me to seek Your Truth._
> _I love You, Lord. Thank You that You … love me, too._
> _Amen._

VIEWER GUIDE: SESSION TWO
COME LIKE A CHILD

We need to FILL up with God every moment of the day! Romans 8:34 says Jesus is praying for us, and He is available 24 hours a day!

* The SIMPLICITY of a Child.

1. CHILDREN seem to be a running theme this week! Jesus said, "Let them come."
Unless we come like CHILDREN, we will not receive the _____ of God.

2. We tend to complicate life. It's hard to let go and let God.

Psalm 46:10, God's Word
"Let go of your concerns! Then you will know that I am God. I rule the nations. I rule the earth."

Adults hesitate. Children JUMP right in. What is stopping you from JUMPING into Jesus' lap?

* God knows our HEARTS, and Jesus accepts us as we are.

3. Jesus is NOT out of touch with our _____. Take the mercy and ask for help! His love for us is unconditional.

Hebrews 4;16, The Message
"Let's walk up to Him and get what He is so ready to give."

* Children are HUMBLE and BELIEVE.

4. Jesus came as a _____ servant and our attitude should be the same. Children want to get to know Jesus because His love is _____.

5. **Greatness** and **humility** work together in God's kingdom. To be great is to be: joyful in hope, patient in affliction, faithful in prayer.

"For God so loved _____ (put your name in), that He gave His only Son that if you BELIEVE in Him, _____ (your name) will not die but have eternal life." John 3:16

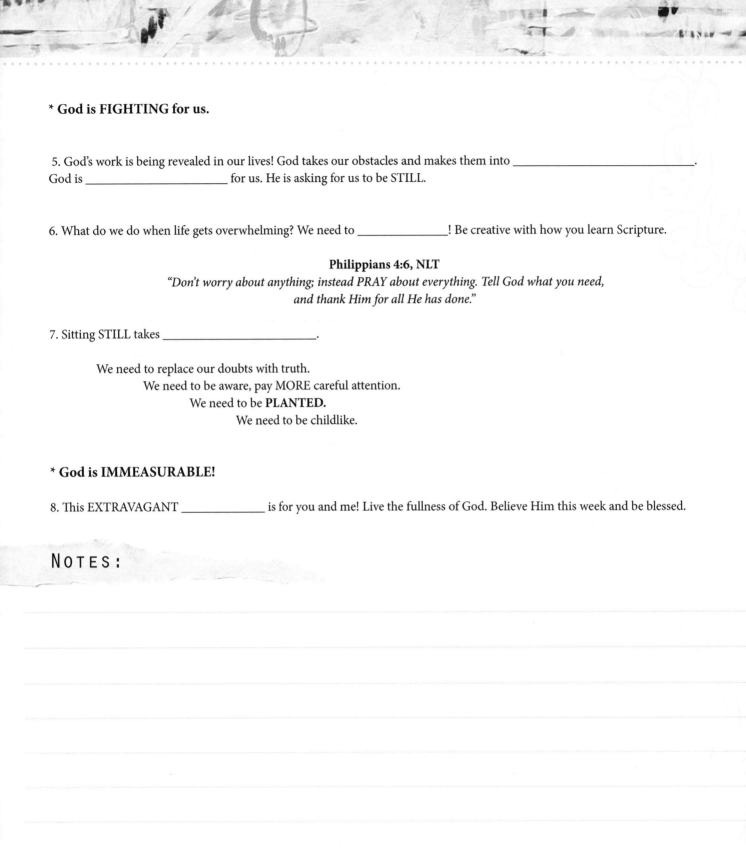

* God is FIGHTING for us.

5. God's work is being revealed in our lives! God takes our obstacles and makes them into _____.
God is _____ for us. He is asking for us to be STILL.

6. What do we do when life gets overwhelming? We need to _____! Be creative with how you learn Scripture.

Philippians 4:6, NLT
"Don't worry about anything; instead PRAY about everything. Tell God what you need,
and thank Him for all He has done."

7. Sitting STILL takes _____.

> We need to replace our doubts with truth.
>> We need to be aware, pay MORE careful attention.
>> We need to be **PLANTED.**
>>> We need to be childlike.

* God is IMMEASURABLE!

8. This EXTRAVAGANT _____ is for you and me! Live the fullness of God. Believe Him this week and be blessed.

N O T E S :

Video sessions are available for download at www.thouartexalted.com/PLANTED ~ teaching videos

WEEK THREE: DAY ONE/ SET TO SIT

Can you believe we are already in week three? There is so much to learn about being **PLANTED** before the Lord. This week we will look at **WHO** sits before the Lord, **WHY** they sit, and the **BENEFITS** and **BLESSINGS** of … **sitting.**

Today, I want to refresh our minds and look at our foundational passage. Read Psalm 1:1-3 from *The Message*.

> *"How well God must like you—*
> *you don't hang out at Sin Saloon,*
> *you don't slink along Dead-End Road,*
> *you don't go to Smart-Mouth College.*
> *Instead you thrill to God's Word,*
> *you chew on Scripture day and night.*
> *You're a tree* **replanted** *in Eden,*
> *bearing fresh fruit every month,*
> *Never dropping a leaf,*
> *always in blossom."*

I have to admit, when I read the phrase **replanted** in Eden, I almost jumped out of my seat. I turned straight to Genesis to the account of the Garden of Eden. Lo and behold, the imagery of trees and streams are abundant! Of course they are.

• **Let's start by reading Genesis 2:4-10.**

> • **What word do you see in Genesis 2:8 that reminds you of our study?**
> _____

> • **How did God place the man He had formed?**
> _____

> • **What about the trees? Please describe them.**
> _____
> _____

> • **What two trees are mentioned in these verses?**
> _____

> • **What flowed in the garden?**
> _____

I think it's fascinating that God chose to use tree images in the beginnings of Scripture. First, the TREE OF LIFE represents "the giving of life, without death, to those who eat its fruit."[1] SECOND, the tree of THE KNOWLEDGE OF GOOD AND EVIL signifies "the giving of knowledge of good and evil ultimately leading to death for those who eat its fruit."[1] And finally, the tree that represents US when we are PLANTED by streams of water (Psalm 1:2).

We have already discussed Eve, the first famous window shopper. Now let's step back in time BEFORE she stood too long in front of the window of temptation … even BEFORE evil entered the world.

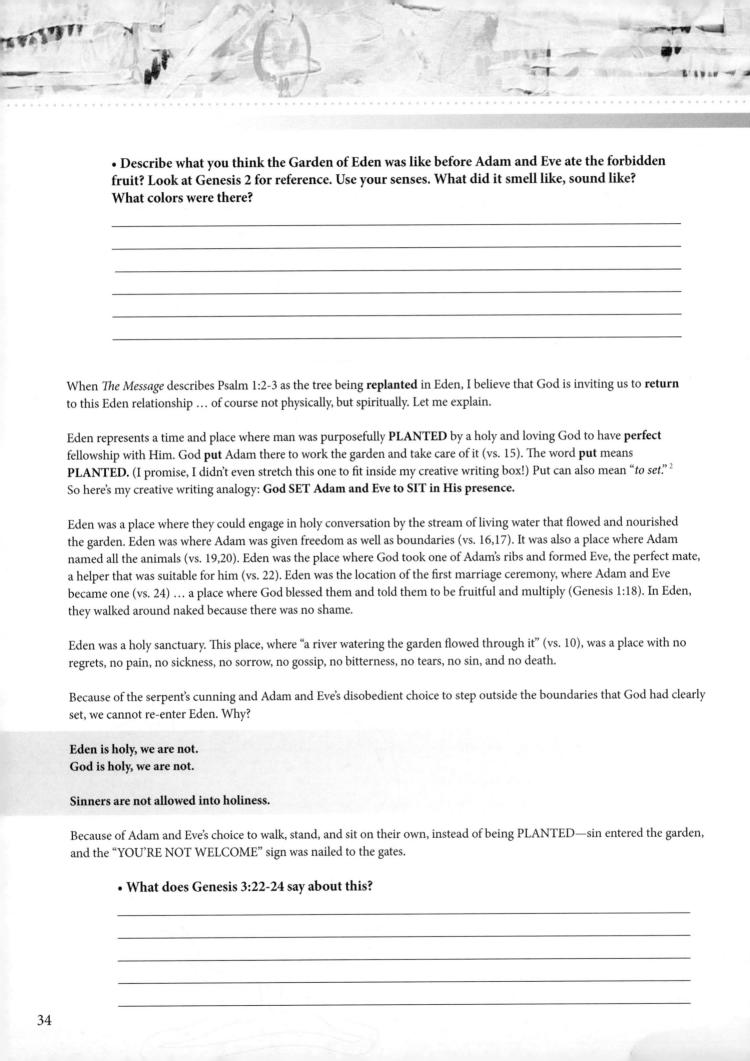

• Describe what you think the Garden of Eden was like before Adam and Eve ate the forbidden fruit? Look at Genesis 2 for reference. Use your senses. What did it smell like, sound like? What colors were there?

_____

_____

_____

_____

_____

_____

When *The Message* describes Psalm 1:2-3 as the tree being **replanted** in Eden, I believe that God is inviting us to **return** to this Eden relationship … of course not physically, but spiritually. Let me explain.

Eden represents a time and place where man was purposefully **PLANTED** by a holy and loving God to have **perfect** fellowship with Him. God **put** Adam there to work the garden and take care of it (vs. 15). The word **put** means **PLANTED.** (I promise, I didn't even stretch this one to fit inside my creative writing box!) Put can also mean "*to set.*" [2] So here's my creative writing analogy: **God SET Adam and Eve to SIT in His presence.**

Eden was a place where they could engage in holy conversation by the stream of living water that flowed and nourished the garden. Eden was where Adam was given freedom as well as boundaries (vs. 16,17). It was also a place where Adam named all the animals (vs. 19,20). Eden was the place where God took one of Adam's ribs and formed Eve, the perfect mate, a helper that was suitable for him (vs. 22). Eden was the location of the first marriage ceremony, where Adam and Eve became one (vs. 24) … a place where God blessed them and told them to be fruitful and multiply (Genesis 1:18). In Eden, they walked around naked because there was no shame.

Eden was a holy sanctuary. This place, where "a river watering the garden flowed through it" (vs. 10), was a place with no regrets, no pain, no sickness, no sorrow, no gossip, no bitterness, no tears, no sin, and no death.

Because of the serpent's cunning and Adam and Eve's disobedient choice to step outside the boundaries that God had clearly set, we cannot re-enter Eden. Why?

Eden is holy, we are not.
God is holy, we are not.

Sinners are not allowed into holiness.

Because of Adam and Eve's choice to walk, stand, and sit on their own, instead of being PLANTED—sin entered the garden, and the "YOU'RE NOT WELCOME" sign was nailed to the gates.

• **What does Genesis 3:22-24 say about this?**

_____

_____

_____

_____

_____

Along with the "Do Not Enter" sign, God hung the sign of **redemption through Jesus Christ**. He did not leave them in an eternal state of no-returns, but initiated **a plan**—a plan to one day **restore** the Eden relationship where men and woman could once again have holy conversations at the river.

Because the blood of Jesus washes away our sin (1 John 1:7-9), we are **RE-INVITED** to be **REPLANTED** in Eden where we can SIT in His presence again. In fact, Scripture says we can come with confidence to the throne of grace (Hebrews 4:16). God invites us to come … to SIT where once again we can lay down our regrets, our pain, our sickness, our sorrow, our battle with gossip or bitterness, and our tears.

I'll close today with this story.

I was visiting Brevard, North Carolina, when a little boy walked up to me, motioned for me to hold out my hand, and proceeded to place his used, chewed-up gum in my palm. What is it about kids? Do they really believe moms are living trash cans? In this case, any mom would have done the job just fine—I just happened to be first in line. Gross. I didn't even know the kid. Then it occurred to me. I give God my used, chewed-up gum all the time. We are born with an emptiness in our souls that can only be filled when we invite Jesus into our lives. No amount of money, pleasure, popularity, prestige, or power will ever satisfy the natural longing we have in our hearts for the Lord. We long for the Savior, who lovingly opens wide His hands and motions us to give Him our soggy, chewed-up lives. In return, He doesn't throw us away, but gives His life so we can have **new life**—a new stick of gum that lasts forever. Willie Wonka can't even beat that! Are you ready to come and sit today and be **replanted in Eden**? The sign that hangs on the east gate now says, **"Come, ALL are welcome!"**

> "But if we LIVE in the light, as God does, we share in life with each other. And the BLOOD of his Son Jesus washes ALL our sins away.
> If we say that we have not sinned, we are fooling ourselves, and the truth isn't in our hearts. But if we CONFESS our sins to God, he can ALWAYS be trusted to FORGIVE us and **take our sins away."**
>
> 1 John 1:7-9
> (CEV)

EXTRA VERSES BY THE STREAM:

• **Do you know that you have been purposefully PLANTED by a holy God who invites you to SIT in His presence?**

• **What do the following verses say about this promise?**

  • **Psalm 138:8**

  _____

  _____

  _____

  • **Philippians 1:6**

  _____

  _____

  _____

  • **Psalm 100:3-5**

  _____

  _____

  _____

DAY TWO/ NO HIDDEN FEES

We have established that we are invited to sit and be replanted in Eden. Now, let's take a look at another Biblical figure that took the time to SIT.

- **Read Luke 10:39.** As you read, add an extra emphasis on the word **sat**. I pray this Scripture will open your day with a whole new meaning.

> "And she had a sister called Mary, who **SAT** at the Lord's feet and **LISTENED** to his teaching." Luke 10:39 (ESV)

Sarah Young writes in her book, *Jesus Calling*, that when we sit in the Lord's presence, we are demonstrating our love for Him.

> "Put aside all that is waiting to be done and refuse to worry about anything. This sacred time together strenghens you and prepares you to face whatever the day will bring."[3]

I understand all too well that sometimes it is **hard** to find time to SIT in the morning—especially when the activities of the day are NOT waiting for you to have a quiet time! I almost can hear the *William Tell Overture* as I get out of bed.

Typical day: Wake up four kids. Did you brush your teeth? Your shorts don't match. No, you have worn those three days in a row. Your shirt has toothpaste on it. Lunches? You forgot to pack them last night? No, you cannot pack three chips and a cookie. Where's the fruit? Mom, please sign this. I need money for the dance. Who fed the chickens? Cat? Dog? The trash needs to be taken out. You can't find your ballet shoes, again? Oh, you wanted coffee? Toast? Yes, I did forget to pick up your pants from the dry cleaners. So sorry. Form? I was supposed to sign something? Sorry again. Let's pray. See you this afternoon. Love you ALL!

Sound familiar?

- **What does your typical morning look like?**

On a side note, if you haven't seen Anita Renfroe's Youtube video about being a busy mom, you NEED to watch it. She's a Christian comedian. (http://www.youtube.com/watch?v=YYukEAmoMCQ)

- **Let's read Proverbs 16:3.**
- **How do you commit your plans to the Lord each day?**

_____

_____

The International Children's Bible (ICB) says,

> *"Depend on the Lord in whatever you do. Then your plans will SUCCEED." Proverbs 16:3*

- **In reviewing Psalm 1:2-3, do you see a parallel between Proverbs 16:3 and Psalm 1:3?**

_____

_____

> "Blessed are those whose delight is IN the law of the LORD; and on his law, he MEDITATES day and night. He is like a TREE PLANTED by streams of water, which yields its FRUIT in season and whose leaf does not wither. WHATEVER he does PROSPERS."
>
> Psalm 1:2-3

• **What happens when we do not depend on the Lord for our day?**

_____

_____

When we take the time to **sit** and **depend** on the Lord for our day, we will prosper. Why? It's both a blessing and a promise from God. We will be blessed when we choose to depend **FIRST** instead of running "feet first" into the business of our day.

> • **Let's go back and look at the entire passage where Mary is sitting at Jesus' feet. We will find proof in Scripture as to why sitting is so necessary. Read Luke 10:38-41.**

> • **Who do we find sitting in this passage? What is she also doing?**

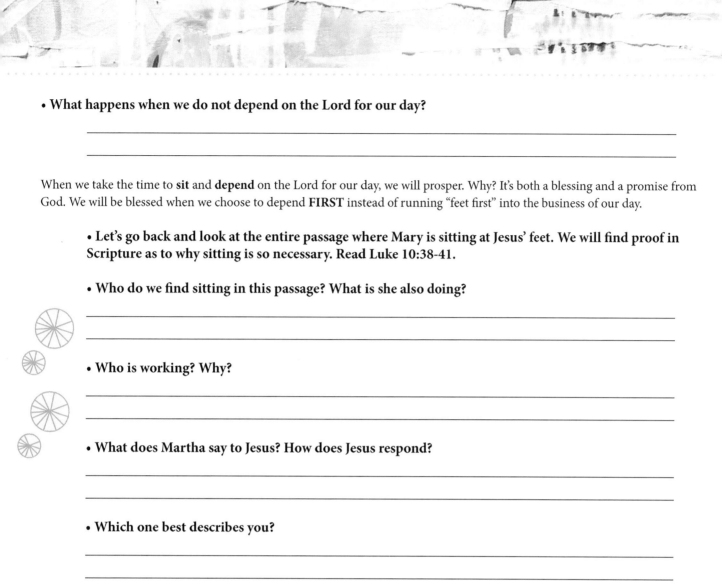

_____

_____

> • **Who is working? Why?**

_____

_____

> • **What does Martha say to Jesus? How does Jesus respond?**

_____

_____

> • **Which one best describes you?**

_____

_____

In this story, we find Mary sitting and Martha sighing. There has been discussion by scholars as to whether Martha was doing something wrong. I personally feel that opening up your home for guests, preparing meals, or cooking is all good. Recently, I had a conversation with a friend that shed some light on this issue. She agreed that Martha was not doing anything wrong. She simply stated that her **timing** in doing it was wrong. She said to me, "Annie, Jesus was IN the living room, her living room!" Let that soak into your soul. Jesus … **was in** … the living room. What would you do if Jesus was teaching in your living room? I sure hope I would drop the lamb chop and **sit** at His feet to listen—like Mary.

What I love about this story is another aspect of **sitting with Jesus**—His response to Martha. With love and tender affection, He told her the truth in **love.**

> "Martha, Martha," the Lord answered, "you are worried and upset about many things, but few things are needed —or indeed only one. Mary has chosen what is better, and it will not be taken away from her." Luke 10:41-42

Luke describes Martha as being distracted. Thayer's Lexicon describes Martha as being "driven out mentally, over-occupied, too busy."[4] Jesus describes Martha as being worried and upset about many things. Does this describe you? I sure can relate.

Again, this is when the enemy can get the best of us. Listen to Martha's complaint. The _King James Version_ gives us a better glimpse into the drama. Imagine the back of her hand on her forehead in exasperation.

> "But Martha was cumbered about much serving, and came to Him and said, 'Lord dost thou not care that my sister hath left me to serve alone? Bid her therefore that she help me.'" Luke 10:40 (KJV)

I can hear the argument now. "Mom, dost thou not care that I hath cleaned the dishes three nights in a row, and she hath left me to serve alone?" We are so self-absorbed, aren't we? Looking out for number one? We get distracted from the most important thing and put all the focus on … ourselves. When we focus on number one, everyone else is clearly in the wrong. Right? Wrong!

• **Put this story on pause and read Ephesians 4:15 from *The Message*:**

"God wants us to **GROW UP,** to know the whole truth and tell it in love—like Christ in everything.
We take our lead from Christ, who is the source of everything we do.
He keeps us in step with each other. His very breath and blood flow through us,
nourishing us so that we will grow up healthy in God, robust in love."

• **When you read this verse, what "golden nugget" do you take away as you compare this with Luke 10:38-42?**

_____

_____

When we come to SIT and listen to the teachings of Jesus, we GROW UP.
When we come to SIT with Jesus, we begin to reflect His nature.
When we come to SIT at Jesus' feet, we must put all distraction aside.
When we come to SIT, we are softened to hear His gentle correction—Jesus speaks Truth and love into our lives where we might need to be corrected.

American Express states that "Membership has its Privileges."™ Jesus says that **Sitting has its Privileges**. Sitting prepares you and strengthens you for the day. Sitting helps you give up your worries and lean on Christ. Sitting makes you GROW UP. I don't know about you, but I'm signing up for "Membership with Jesus." And by the way, there are no hidden fees.

DAY THREE/ THE MASTER SILVERSMITH

Let's begin today by looking at a very interesting verse about **SITTING.**

"He will sit as a refiner and a purifier of silver.
He will purify the Levites
and refine them like gold and silver.
They will belong to the Lord,
presenting a righteous offering."
Malachi 3:3 (CEB)

• **Who is the One sitting in this passage from Malachi? What is He doing?**

_____

_____

When a silversmith places a piece of silver over the fire, he purposefully places it over the hottest part to burn away all the impurities. The heat releases the dross, the contaminant, to allow the metal to take its new form. It is also true that a "good refiner never leaves the crucible, but will **sit** down by it so the fire will not become even one degree too hot and possibly harm the metal. And as soon as he skims the last bit of dross away from the surface and sees His face **reflected** in the pure metal, he extinguishes the fire."[5]

Can you see the **connection** God has with the master silversmith? He, too, never leaves His sitting position by the fire of our circumstances and is always making sure the fire never gets **too hot**.

> • **What evidence do you see from the following verses that the Lord SITS by us and NEVER leaves His position overseeing us? What are the personal promises we can stand on?**

> • **1 Corinthians 10:13**

_____

_____

> • **Psalm 139:1-4**

_____

_____

> • **Psalm 121:3-8**

_____

_____

"So LET God work his will in you. Yell a loud **NO** to the devil and watch him scamper. Say a quiet **YES** to God and he'll be there in no time. Quit dabbling in sin. Purify your inner life. Quit playing the field. Hit bottom, and cry your eyes out. The fun and games are over. Get SERIOUS, really serious.

Get down on your knees before the Master; it's the only way you'll get on your feet."

James 4:7-10 (MSG)

I love the imagery in Exodus 14:21 where Moses is leading the Israelites through the Red Sea.

> "Then Moses stretched out his hand over the sea, and ALL that night THE LORD drove the sea back with a strong east wind and turned it into dry land. The waters were divided, and the Israelites went through the sea on dry ground, with a wall of water on their right and on their left."

Have there been times in your life when you felt like there was a huge wall of trouble on both your right and your left? Rest assured, you have a GOD who never leaves His post. He is holding out His arms ALL NIGHT LONG. He is sitting by the crucible wheel using your trial to purify you and release your impurities to make you **stronger**. He is driving back the wind and waters leading you onward to dry land.

> • **What does James 1:2-4 say about enduring trials?**

_____

_____

James 4:7 says:

> "Submit yourselves, then, to God. Resist the devil, and he will flee from you. Come near to God and He will come near to you."

It's not easy or fun to be refined in the fire.

Let me take you back to Halloween, 2001. My daughter was three-years old and was dressing up as her toy poodle's mommy, "Poochie." You know, the pink battery-operated poodles that walk, bark, then do a back flip? Daley was going as Poochie's mommy. Go figure. Now you might be asking the same question as I was. What does a "Poochie mommy" wear? I traveled all over Jacksonville trying to find the **perfect** pink top, pink boa collar, and pink pants to match.

Pause—At this point in my life, I was involved in Bible Study Fellowship. This particular day, I was volunteering in the children's program. We were studying about casting our worries unto the Lord. The leaders told the children to hold out their arms and visually put their worries in the palm of their hands. From there, they would throw up their hands as if they were casting their cares to the Lord. I thought this was a great idea and decided to share it with my three-year old, aka: Poochie's mommy.

As Halloween day dawned, Daley decided she no longer wanted to be Poochie's mommy. Oh, NO! Poochie's mommy's mommy had driven all over town putting together an original "Poochie mommy" costume! I firmly explained to her, "Daley, you **ARE** going to be Poochie's mommy!" Oh, boy. That's when the furnace got hot and some refining was needed.

Daley looked at me and said, "Mommy, hold out your hand." She cupped my hand and said, "Now put your worry in here and cast it off to the Lord!" I didn't know whether to drop-kick the battery-operated poodle across the room or to burst out in laughter! I opted for the latter. What a lesson I had learned that day. Why do we get so heated when we cannot control the outcome of our lives—much less our children's Halloween costume? Start heatin' up the furnace.

As we draw near to God each day and surrender our agendas, God is **refining** us in order to see His reflection **in** us. Today, we see that God is **sitting,** too. He never sleeps and is **always** watching over us. He keeps us from harm and is **always** looking out for our best. He never gives us more than what we can bear and **always** provides a way out. Even when the waters rage around us, we can feel the peace that surpasses all understanding (Philippians 4:6-7) because He promises us He will never leave us nor forsake us (Hebrews 13:5).

- **As we close today, meditate on Psalm 139:23-24.**

> "SEARCH me, God, and know my heart;
> TEST me and know my anxious thoughts.
> SEE if there is any offensive way in me,
> and LEAD me in the way everlasting."

What in your life might need to be purified by the Lord's fire? Where do you need God to do a little **probing** to see if you have anxious thoughts or offensive ways? I think we might be sitting a little longer today! The sweet promise is that as you SIT and LISTEN, His Truth in love will speak clearly into your heart. Sitting is a place of reflection, as well as the place of refinement, preparing us to better glorify Him and **reflect His image**.

Remember the **sage words** of Poochie's mommy: "Cast your cares unto Him" **before** you feel the rising temperature of the furnace!

DAY FOUR/ POWER UP SOME HEAVEN

I want to dedicate the next two days to the **teachings of Jesus.** In Scripture, we see instances of Jesus sitting, the disciples sitting, the people of Israel sitting, and the final seating of Jesus by the right hand of God. My prayer is that as we look at these stories together, we can personally identify with the **benefits and blessings** of taking the **time** to intentionally **sit** with the Lord.

- **Let's begin by looking at John 6:1-13.**

- **Identify the two times the word SITTING is used in the passage. Describe who was sitting and what was happening.**

_____

_____

The FIRST place we see the word SIT in this passage, Jesus is SITTING with his disciples. Isn't this just like Him? Here the word means "*to dwell, to be seated.*" Jesus was their leader and their Savior, but He was also their **friend**. He wants to be our friend, too—and not just on Facebook.

> • **Read John 15:14-17. What does this verse say about Jesus being our friend?**

_____

_____

> • **What does Jesus reveal to us when we sit with Him? What does He promise to us?**

_____

_____

_____

"You are my FRIENDS when you do the things I command you. I'm no longer calling you servants because servants don't understand what their master is thinking and planning. No, I've named you FRIENDS because I've let you in on EVERYTHING I've heard from the Father. You didn't choose me, remember; **I chose you,** *and put you in the world to bear FRUIT, fruit that* **won't spoil.** *As fruit bearers, whatever you ask the Father in relation to me, he gives you. But remember the ROOT command:* **Love one another."**

John 15:14-17 (MSG)

I have included *The Message* translation to the left because it is teaming with **tree analogy**. Can you see it?

When we SIT with Jesus, He "lets us in on EVERYTHING He's heard from the Father." He chose us and PUT us into the world to bear FRUIT, fruit that would not spoil. (I hope by now your thoughts are automatically reflecting back to the first Psalm where we yield our fruit in season, our leaf will not wither, and whatever we do will prosper.) Jesus ends His teaching with this "**ROOT command: Love one another.**"

The SECOND place we see the word SIT is in John 6:10. Jesus tells the people to SIT.

> • **What is the first thing Jesus does when all the people are seated on the grassy slopes?**

_____

_____

He takes the bread and gives **thanks**. Next, He gives the people, who are seated, as much as they want.

> "Then Jesus took the bread and, having given THANKS, gave it to those who were
> SEATED. He did the same with the fish. All ate as much as they wanted."
> John 6:11 (MSG)

I have to stop and tell you I am completely overwhelmed by the powerful fact that Jesus wants to be my friend and wants to tell me ALL the things the Father told Him. Just as He SAT with the disciples, He wants to SIT with me. Just as He invited the people to SIT and watch the miracle He was about to perform, He invites me to SIT and watch what He can do in my life when I **believe**. Jesus wants to reveal to me the mysteries of Scripture. He wants to fill me with a fruitful life to love and serve Him. He wants and INVITES me to SIT with Him. He chose me. He feeds me His Word. He gives thanks for me. And He gives thanks for you, too.

> • **How does this Scripture touch your soul? (John 6:11)**

_____

_____

41

- **Let's read Ephesians 3:20-21.**

- **Do you believe God can do more than you can ask or imagine? What do you need to believe Him for today?**

_____

_____

I have always been intrigued by the part in the verse where it says, "… according to His power that is at work within [you]." Have you ever seen the movie *Monsters, Inc.*? The film is about monsters that live in another realm called Monstropolis. In order to **power up** this world, they have to scare people in our world. The more scary they are, the more power they generate in Monstropolis. This might be a silly comparison and not too theological, but I like to think that my belief in Jesus makes God proud and somehow "powers up" the heavenlies. Go with me here. When I SIT and **believe** that Jesus can do beyond what I could ever expect or imagine, I am **believing** that He is who He says He is. I am believing He is alive in me, He is interceding for me at the right hand of God (day five), and He considers ME to be His friend. Wow. Now that's some power!

- **Let's quickly look at James 1:5. What does God give us when we ask?** _____

Yes, God gives us **wisdom**. Compare and delight on the different translations of Proverbs 1:7.

"The FEAR of the LORD is the BEGINNING of WISDOM." (NIV)

"Fear of the LORD is the FOUNDATION of TRUE KNOWLEDGE, but fools despise wisdom and discipline." (NLT)

"KNOWLEDGE begins with RESPECT for the LORD. But foolish people HATE wisdom and self-control." (ICB)

Fear in this verse does not mean the same as the scary monsters in *Monsters, Inc.* Fear is a holy reverence, a holy respect—the foundation of true knowledge. **Knowledge** can be read as a knowledge of GOD, an understanding of who He is. When we come by the river to SIT, to be REPLANTED in Eden, to have holy conversations, we are **sitting** in the presence of the King of Kings where we are growing in true knowledge. We are sitting with Jesus … who teaches us how to trust … who calls us His friend … who desires us to bear fruit … who wants to power us up with belief … and who will never, EVER leave our side. Where are you today? Are you being foolish—despising God's wisdom and "listening to the wicked, going where sinners go, or doing what bad people do" (Psalm 1:1, ICB)? Or are you embracing God's wisdom and intentionally sitting with Him, allowing His power to work within you? Let's not get up until we are **fueled with peace and blessing.** Let's get busy **sitting**, learning, fearing, respecting, knowing, and **power up some Heaven!**

Let's close today by praying the Scripture from Ephesians 5:15-17.

Lord, I pray to be careful in how I live, not as unwise, but as wise. I pray to make the most of every opportunity because the days are busy and distracting. I pray not to live the foolish life, but rather to understand what Your will is for me. I pray to be filled with the fullness of Your Spirit so You can lead me and teach me the way to go. Teach me, O Lord, to always give thanks like You taught us when You fed over 5000 people with five fish and two loaves of bread. You can do far more than I could ever expect or imagine. I want to believe that today. I want to believe You are the beginning of wisdom and knowledge. May the glory and the power of Jesus light up my life today. I pray all who see me would see something different because You are shining in my life. May I look like a beautiful, strong, and faithful tree today—swaying in the sunlight of Your purpose and promise. Amen.

"Now to him who IS ABLE to do IMMEASURABLY MORE than all we ASK or IMAGINE, according to his POWER that is at work WITHIN us, to HIM be GLORY in the church and in CHRIST JESUS throughout all generations, for ever and ever! Amen."

Ephesians 3:20-21

DAY FIVE/ JESUS SITTING

It's day five. Great job this week! I know we have looked at **a lot** of Scripture. I pray that, as you are SITTING in this study, you are **growing** in your faith. Today, we are going to look at another time when Jesus **sat down.** However, this was the last and final curtain call. He sits forever by the right hand side of God. Let's get cozy by the river and begin with looking at the definition of **SIT.**

> TO SIT: "to rest on the buttocks or haunches, to hold a session, to cover eggs for hatching, roost, perch, to have a location."[6]

Funny, huh?

I doubt many of us are covering our eggs for hatching. Heck, I am still trying to figure out how to use "haunch" in a sentence! I guess I don't use my SAT words often.

- **Let's open our Bibles and look at Hebrews 1:1-3.**

  - **How is Jesus described in these passages?**

  _____

  _____

  - **Where is Jesus now, and what did He DO to be able to sit there?**

  _____

  _____

Before the life, death, and resurrection of Christ, the Jewish people worshipped in the temple and offered animal sacrifices to make atonement for their sins. Atonement simply means the forgiveness or covering of one's sin. The word **sin** comes from an ancient archery term meaning to "miss the perfect mark." When an archer missed hitting the bulls-eye, he was said to have "sinned." Any shot outside the bulls-eye was considered a "sin." As we have discussed, we, too, miss the perfect mark of the holiness of God because we have a sinful nature. A blood sacrifice was required by God in the Old Testament because life is in the blood (Leviticus 17:11). A blood sacrifice was required by God to cover over sin. **Life covering over death.** However, this animal sacrifice was only temporary. Jesus came to earth as the **permanent** sacrificial lamb. His death on the cross and the shedding of His blood covered our sin **once and for all.** Romans 6:23 says:

> "For the wages of sin is death, but the gift of God is eternal life in Christ Jesus our Lord."

The penalty for our sin is death. But the life of Christ **covers over** and **forgives** our sin ONCE AND FOR ALL. Romans 3:22 reminds us the only way we can become right with God is to receive Jesus through faith. We ALL fall short of the glory of God, and we ALL miss that perfect mark. But there is **great news**!

> "But God demonstrated His love for us in that while we were yet sinners, Christ died for us." Romans 5:8

- **Read Romans 5:1-5.**

  - **How are we justified–declaring to be righteous or holy before God?**

  _____

  _____

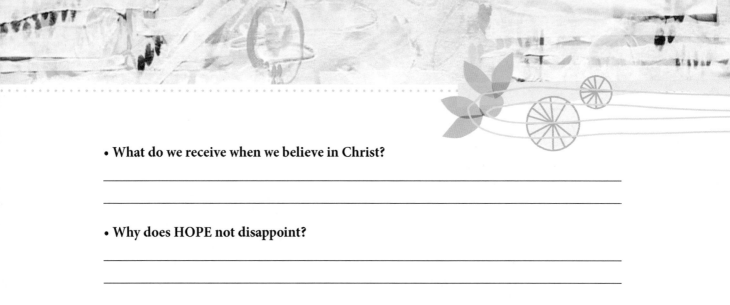

• **What do we receive when we believe in Christ?**

_____

_____

• **Why does HOPE not disappoint?**

_____

_____

We receive **peace** with God, **access** into the grace of God, and **hope** of the glory of God. Romans 5:1-11 is a good place to take time to SIT and ponder. These verses are the foundations of our Christian faith and the central reasoning behind SITTING before the Lord, which we will discuss in detail next week.

• **Let's read Hebrews 10:11-18 from** *The Message:*

> "Every priest goes to work at the altar EACH day, offers the SAME OLD sacrifices year in, year out, and never makes a dent in the sin problem. As a priest, Christ made a SINGLE sacrifice for sins, and that was it! Then HE SAT DOWN RIGHT BESIDE GOD and waited for his enemies to cave in. It was a PERFECT SACRIFICE by a PERFECT PERSON to PERFECT some very imperfect people. By that single offering, he did EVERYTHING that needed to be done for EVERYONE who takes part in the purifying process."

That, my friends, is **POWER**! I think Heaven is experiencing some high voltage right now! Can you imagine the rejoicing when someone is PERFECTED in Christ the moment they believe? Luke 15:7 says there is MORE rejoicing in Heaven over one lost sinner who repents and returns to God than over ninety-nine others who are righteous and haven't strayed away!

Yes, Jesus SAT down, **once and for all**. His mission was complete. Yet, we STILL find Him very much active and ALIVE in our lives today.

> "Who then will condemn us? No one--for Christ Jesus DIED for us and was RAISED to life for us, and he is SITTING in the place of honor at God's right hand, PLEADING for us."
>
> Romans 8:34
> (NLT)

• **Read Romans 8:34. What is He actively doing right now?**

_____

_____

Christ is seated in honor by the right hand of God, and He is actively **praying** for us—right now. Rest in this promise today. Whatever you may be struggling with, Jesus is constantly pleading on your behalf.

EXTRA VERSES BY THE STREAM:

Look up these promises in Scripture which confirm our belief that God not only **hears** us, but also **answers** our prayers.

• **What do the following Scriptures say about God HEARING our prayers?**

• **Psalm 116:1**

_____

_____

• **Psalm 6:9**

_____

_____

• **Psalm 66:19**

_____

_____

• **What do the following Scriptures say about God ANSWERING our prayers?**

• **Psalm 138:3**

_____

_____

• **John 14:13-14**

_____

_____

• **Psalm 118:5**

_____

_____

We did it! We finished another great week together. We have studied Mary, Martha, the disciples, the Jewish people, our own lives, God, and Jesus Himself in ALL different aspects of SITTING. Next week, we will explore **HOW** we sit with the Lord. Thank you for being a part of this journey with me. I, too, am learning the blessings and privileges that come when we take the initiative to **SIT** at the feet of Jesus.

"Let us hold **unswervingly** to the HOPE we profess, for HE who PROMISED is faithful."

Hebrews 10:23

Let me share a sweet testimony in closing. I was with a friend named Kyle last night who shared with me her usual morning routine of waking up at 4:30 to workout. Yes, AM not PM. She went on to tell me that one particular morning, she decided to **sit** with the Lord instead of going to the gym. Her face lit up when she told me how God spoke into her heart and gave her certain wisdom and discernment she had not felt in a long time. She experienced the peace and blessings of God when she delighted and meditated on His Word! She is a fine example of a beautiful tree, drinking from the stream of Living Water, being filled to the fullness of HIM!

I'll end by praying over us.

Father, I pray today we would hold tightly to all we have learned this week.
We trust in Your promises and believe in Your Son. As we go forward this week, I pray we
can be found replanted in Eden, delighting in Your holy presence. I pray we can be found sitting
at the feet of Your teaching while listening and not being distracted with the busyness of our lives.
I pray we can be molded to Your ways as a Master Silversmith forms his most precious creations.
Finally, O Lord, I pray we can SIT and give thanks. I pray we would confess where we fall short and
believe in Your grace to step forward with confidence, knowing You are SEATED in Heaven praying for us.
We love You with all that we are. Amen.

VIEWER GUIDE: SESSION THREE
RE-INVITED TO SIT WITH GOD

"But God demonstrates His own love for us in this: While we were still sinners, Christ died for us."

Romans 5:8

You are a tree RE-PLANTED in Eden!

1. When Adam and Eve disobeyed God, sin distroyed a perfect, holy relationship with God. They were cast from the garden of Eden, but not without a plan. God ALWAYS has a _____. Jesus reinvites us to be RE -_____ into a relationship with God.

2. The "You-Are-Not-Welcome" sign has been changed to the "_____ are WELCOME."

THREE QUESTIONS to ASK:
- **How do we know we are welcome?**
- **How do we know we have been RE-INVITED to be RE-PLANTED?**
- **What do we need to bring to the party?**

3. We are welcomed back into the holiness of God because GOD has demonstrated His Love for us that while we were sinners, Christ _____ for us.

4. We have been re-invited and re-PLANTED to come back to Eden because Jesus has invited us.

5. The only "casserole" we need to bring to the party is _____.

6. We will never know the plans God has for us unless we come to _____. God reveals Himself to us when we are focused on Him.

Proverbs 16:3
"Commit your way to the Lord, then your plans will succeed."

When you are committing your day to the Lord, you are leaving the _____ up to Him. You are surrendering your agenda to Him.

7. **HOW DO WE MEASURE SUCCESS?** We measure our success by _____ our agendas and _____ our day to the Lord.

8. We need to SIT and LISTEN to what the Lord wants to teach us. We need to STOP, DROP, and SIT. People will recognize it when we are PLANTED by the Lord. Life gets turned upside down fast! We need to be PLANTED and trust in the Lord.

9. We are robbed from the MOMENT when we are _____ by tomorrow.

    • Our SUCCESS is not based on our day. Our SUCCESS is based on the PEACE we receive from a holy God who has invited us to be re-planted in the garden.

10. We sit so Jesus can TEACH us. We SIT to _____.

    God is FAITHFUL. God KNOWS all our ways. God WATCHES over us.

11. Trials _____ us. We reflect the image of Christ. God never wastes ANYTHING. Our trials always have a purpose.

A TREE CAN'T GROW UP UNTIL IT GROWS _____.

JESUS COVERS US. Jesus covers our unholiness when we believe in Him.

NOTES:

Key to Lesson: Plan, Planted, All, Died, Belief, Sit, Results, Surrendering, Committing, Distracted, Commit, Purify, Down

Video sessions are available for download at www.thouartexalted.com/PLANTED ~ teaching videos

47

Taking a quick look back, we have seen what it looks like to be invited to **SIT** with the Lord. We have also looked at characters in the Bible who were **blessed** as they sat. This week we will be looking at **HOW we should sit** … in patience, in prayer, and in persistence seeking the presence and strength of God.

For the next two days, we will focus on **Proverbs 19:11.**

"A man's WISDOM gives him PATIENCE, it is to his glory to OVERLOOK an offense."

Let's begin by asking ourselves, "Why do we come to the river?" Is it because we are promised to be the image of a strong Christian woman where our fruit yields in season? Is it because we will be strengthened during the storms of life where our faith will not wither? Is it because by seeking the Lord's will we will be prosperous? Is it to grow in our relationship with the Lord? Is it to check off our quiet-time box? Why? **Why do you come?**

I pray as you study this week, you will be given at least one concrete answer each day as to **why** you come to the river. I can't wait to share these with you!

As I write this, I can hear my kids arguing.

"What did I do?" Winnie questioned. "You messed it ALL up!" they humphed. I think Winnie must have sat on the remote control switching stations on the boys. Big deal? Not really. Then why were they so quick to react? Why were they so quick and harsh with their words? I could hear her say, "I'm sorry guys, okay?" I knew she felt terrible, but their words only made her feel **worse**. Was sitting on the remote a mistake? Yes. Was their tone of voice? No.

Think back to week one—**We ALL have a choice.**
Proverbs 19:11 says, "It is to his glory to overlook an offense." Whose glory are we talking about? Man's glory or God's glory? I think both. When we give the offense to God, we are essentially giving Him the glory. We will find that surrendering this control takes trust, wisdom, and **patience.**

> • **Do you easily overlook someone's offense, or do you keep a grudge and hold it against them?**

_____

_____

I believe patience is the ability to look **beyond** someone's offense. This is not always easy. This is the reason why we need to take our cares and concerns to the river, releasing it to God and trusting Him to handle it before our selfish reactions get in the way. Have you heard this quote by Chuck Swindoll? "Life is 10 percent what happens to [us] and 90 percent of how [you] react to it."[1] How true.

> • **What do you think is the opposite of patience?**

_____

I believe the opposite of patience is the compulsion to **control**. It's the "I'm-going-to-handle-this-myself" attitude. The opposite of patience is refusing to wait for God's hand and deciding to take care of it ourselves.

> "The remarkable thing is we have a choice everyday regarding the ATTITUDE we will embrace for that day. We cannot change our past... we cannot change the fact that people will act in a certain way. We cannot change the inevitable. The only thing we can do is play on the one string we have, and that is our attitude. I am convinced that life is 10% what happens to me and 90% of how I react to it."
>
> -Charles Swindoll

This person is usually characterized by a quick temper and selfish motivation—spouting words she doesn't mean and often regretting it later. I believe true wisdom and patience is knowing **when** to stop. Patience is also learning when to wait, when to pray, and when to **let it go.**

- **Why do you think it is to a person's glory to overlook on offense?**

When you act in faith and trust, you are representing your Heavenly Father. You are reflecting His very character. I remember my parents always telling me, "Annie, your actions represent us." Our actions also personify our Lord.

- **Let's read John 18:15-18 and John 18:25-27.**

  - **Who and what did Peter deny in these verses?**

    _____

    _____

  - **How many times did Peter deny Jesus?**

    _____

- **Now let's look at John 21:12-19.**

  - **How many times did Jesus address Peter with the question about his love for Him?**

    _____

    _____

  - **Did Jesus' patience bring glory to God? How?**

    _____

    _____

  - **How can we learn by Jesus' example?**

    _____

    _____

I don't know about you, but I would have been pretty upset if my right-hand man lied about even knowing me while I was being tried for blasphemy. Yet we see Jesus addressing Peter in the same manner He addressed Martha. He spoke the Truth in love and gave the Father all the glory through His wisdom and patience.

- **Can you think of a situation when you were patient even though someone offended you? What was the outcome?**

You may be wondering why I started with John 21:12. It is because we find Jesus eating breakfast on the beach with His disciples. None of them dared question who He was. Why? Because they **KNEW** it was the LORD. The long days of sitting under His teaching left them with ZERO doubt. When we come and have breakfast with the Lord, sitting by the stream of Living Water, soaking up His wisdom, patience, and power—we, too, know it's Him. We recognize Jesus because we have spent **time** with Him. When we are in the heat of confrontation, it is only through His power working in us that gives us patience and wisdom.

On our own, we work from a place of control and selfish motivation. I know this to be true. When I act out of a quick temper, it becomes clear that Jesus was not invited to my breakfast table. But when I ask Him to join me in the morning and **allow Him** continual access into my heart throughout the day, you better believe I notice it's HIM. Everyone else does too. On my own, I am just little 'ole Annie. In Christ, I can do all things through His strength, helping me to overlook offenses and teaching me to be patient (Philippians 4:13).

Wisdom gives us patience—especially when we have breakfast with the Lord. A good breakfast always makes the day go better, don't you think? Especially if it's french toast!

In closing, it occurred to me that Jesus is in the business of **overlooking** offenses.

> • **Can you think of examples in the Bible where Jesus overlooked offenses and offered a full meal of forgiveness, patience, grace, and wisdom?**
>
> Think about the Samaritan woman. (John 4:4-26)
> Think about the woman caught in adultery and the unbelief of the Jewish leaders. (John 8:1-11)
> Think about Zacchaeus. (Luke 19:1-10)
> Think about Nicodemus. (John 3:1-21)
> Think about Doubting Thomas. (John 20:24-31)
> Think about the bleeding woman. (Luke 8:40-48)
> Think about the criminals who were crucified next to Jesus …
> > "Father, forgive them, for they do not know what they do." Luke 23:32-43
>
> These are just a few examples. Jesus is our prime example of wisdom and patience when overlooking an offense.
>
> **How about you? What does Jesus' example teach you about overlooking an offense?**
>
> _____
> _____
> _____

Today we have learned one of the reasons why we come to the river. We come to learn patience and wisdom to forgive and surrender our control and selfish motives. Let's have some french toast with the Lord, shall we? It will be delicious!

DAY TWO/ RISE YE UP!

I always enjoy looking into different translations of verses and meditating on each one. It never ceases to amaze me how God's Word comes alive in so many new ways.

> • **For example, let's look at the different translations of Proverbs 19:11.**
>
> "A man's DISCRETION makes him SLOW to anger. It is to his glory to OVERLOOK an offense." (NASB)
>
> "SENSIBLE people CONTROL their ANGER, they earn RESPECT by OVERLOOKING wrongs." (NLB)
>
> "Smart people know how to HOLD their tongue, their grandeur is to FORGIVE and FORGET." (TM)

Look at the NASB translation of Proverbs 19:11. "A man's discretion makes him slow to anger." Let's dissect each word.

> **Discretion** means: "insight, caution, preference, understanding."
> **Slow** means: "defer, unhurried, prolong, pokey, leisurely."
> **Anger** means: "rage, irritation, ill-temper, aggravation, peeve, get someone's dander up."[2]

> • **Using the different definitions of these three words, how would you rewrite this verse?**

A man's _____ (discretion) makes him _____ (slow) to _____ (anger).

You could creatively write this verse a couple of ways, but the end result is the same. This person has A LOT of patience. On a side note, I found it interesting that the word for anger can also refer to the nose or nostrils, the place where one breathes. Hmmmm. Did your mom ever tell you to take a deep breath and count to ten as a means to control your anger? You can almost tell when someone is angry just by the flaring of their nostrils. Here's another fun exercise.

> • **Patience can mean slow to anger. What two words would you use in this equation after reading the above definitions of slow and anger?**

_____ + _____ = PATIENCE

I like unhurried aggravation = patience. I also like pokey to peeve = patience.

While patience is a key point in Proverbs 19:11, let's switch our attention to the word **overlook**.

> To overlook means: "to pass over, forgive, to cross over as of a stream."[3]

This speaks volumes to me! We need to take our deferred anger to the stream of the Living Water and let it go … pass it on … let the river carry it away … taking it to God, trusting Him with the outcome.

Let's look at two Bible stories where **crossing over** a body of water signified leaving the past behind and trusting in God for the freedom of the future.

> • **Read Exodus 14:10-31.**

> > • **What did the Israelites have to do to escape from the Egyptians?**
> >
> > _____
> > _____

> > • **How did they trust God?**
> >
> > _____
> > _____
> > _____

> > • **How did God prove His faithfulness?**
> >
> > _____
> > _____
> > _____

"But the Israelites went through the sea on dry ground, with a wall of WATER on their right and on their left. That day the Lord SAVED Israel from the hands of the Egyptians.... And when the Israelites saw the MIGHTY hand of the Lord displayed against the Egyptians, the people FEARED the Lord and put their TRUST in Him and in Moses His servant."

Exodus 14: 29-31

The Israelites had to **cross over** the Red Sea and **leave their past behind.** God was forging their future freedom and releasing them from 400 years of captivity. This took some serious **trust** on their part. Imagine the scene! You may not have been imprisoned for 400 years, but I'm sure many of you have felt like it. When we hold onto our past anger and offenses, we will never experience the **freedom** that God has for us.

51

- **Let's read Joshua 3:5-17.**

    - **What amazing thing happened when the priests reached the flooding waters of the Jordan? (vs. 15-17)**

    _____

    _____

Here again, we see God's faithfulness. This time, the people of Israel had been wandering the desert for 40 years because of their unbelief in the faithfulness of God. Through Joshua, God decides once again to lead them into freedom. What does He choose as a bridge to that freedom? You got it. WATER. Cool, huh?

- **Read Deuteronomy 2:24.**

I have to quote the Kings James Version because of the impact in the reading.

> "RISE ye UP, TAKE your JOURNEY and CROSS OVER the RIVER ..."

Remember, the word **"cross over"** is the same word used in Proverbs 19:11. It means to **overlook.**

The Lord will do amazing things among you ... you just need to **cross over.** Again, it's our choice. Our journey is laden with choices of continual patience, deferring our anger, and letting go. Often we need to let go of something that has held us captive for some time. When we come to the river and ask God to wash away our anger, our bitterness, and our control, we will be bringing glory to Him and releasing ourselves from years of bondage. When we **sit** with Him, our **stand** will be confident in the promise of the freedom He offers. We will, in turn, be **walking** in joy.

If I had a visual for this type of tree, I would see her leaning over the bank each morning to do her laundry ... dirty laundry. Every morning. Praying for wisdom and patience. Praying for discernment to overlook offenses—to see beyond other's sins and to see as God sees. She would see as Jesus saw Peter, overlooking his offense, knowing what he could **become.**

Rise YE UP! Take your journey (your dirty laundry) and cross over the river ... there is freedom on the other side.

DAY THREE/ PATIENT PANCAKES

I hope you have discovered that **patience** plays a leading role when coming to **SIT** at the river. Patience is the fertilizer that makes our trees grow strong in the Lord.

- **What did you learn in day one and two about patience?**

    _____

    _____

Today we will look at two areas that can be tough for all of us ... our speech and our stillness. Let's look at our speech first. Patience is often linked in Scripture with the way we talk to people. I wonder why? (I am smiling right now.)

- **Let's start by reading Proverbs 25:15.**

> "Through PATIENCE a ruler can be persuaded and a GENTLE tongue can break a bone."

• Why do you think we get more accomplished when we have a gentle tongue?

_____

_____

• Looking up the following passages. What do you learn about the tongue? How is our speech connected with patience?

• Proverbs 14:29

_____

_____

• Proverbs 15:1

_____

_____

• Proverbs 15:18

_____

_____

• Proverbs 16:32

_____

_____

Ecclesiastes 7:8-9 says:

> "The end of a matter is BETTER than its beginning and PATIENCE is BETTER than PRIDE."

Oh, the pride. When we give in to our outbursts, we are giving into our need to control. When we are in control, we are being driven by pride. Yuck. When we have an uncontrollable tongue, we are forfeiting the wisdom and the patience we have learned sitting at the river.

Sitting requires that we are STILL.

We must sit still enough to see the reflection of Christ in the river.
We must sit still enough to have a controlled tongue.
We must sit still enough to be patient.

• **Read Psalm 37:7.**

"Be _____ before the Lord and wait _____ for Him. Don't _____ when men succeed in their ways, when they carry out their wicked schemes." (NIV)

Here we see patience again. The NASB says, "**Rest** in the Lord and wait patiently for Him." How do we receive this patience and rest? Yes, by **sitting STILL!**

It was a beautiful morning for making pancakes. There was only **one** problem—we needed another egg. No problem! Why? In addition to our crazy "six-mix," we also have chickens in the back yard. Therefore, we have eggs to our liking each morning. As I was mixing the well-known ingredients of flour, baking soda, salt, oil, and milk, I asked my six-year old to go outside and gather an egg to make our breakfast complete. "Sure, Mom," John John said with gusto as he ran to the chicken coop. After five minutes had passed, I noticed John had not come back with our well sought-out egg. I mean, by this time there either **is** an egg or there is **not** an egg. I peered out the back door and barely made out his little figure. "John John, are there any eggs?" I asked. I could see him standing right at the edge of the coop and heard this reply:

"I'm waiting!"

Oh my! No chicken in her right mind is going to lay an egg while a six-year old is staring her down waiting for this one, very important ingredient for his pancakes.

> Samuel Dickey Gordon says "waiting is much more difficult than walking because waiting requires patience, and patience is a rare virtue"[4]

This week, let's **rest** in the Lord's presence. Today at the riverbank, I pray you will find stillness, quiet speech, great understanding, calm, and perhaps … even a couple of eggs.

DAY FOUR/ DON'T MOVE

Today, I am going to begin with a reading from one my favorite devotionals, *Streams in the Desert.*[5]

> "Once we learn to wait for the Lord's leading in everything, we will know the strength that finds its highest point in an even and steady walk. Waiting ~ keeping yourself faithful to His leading ~ this is the secret of strength."
> Samuel Dickey Gordon

> "Victory is to be won by standing quietly still and waiting. It requires much more courage to stand and wait and still not lose heart or hope, to submit to the will of God, to give up opportunities for work and leave honors to others, and to be quiet, confident, and rejoicing while the other busy multitude goes on happily along their way."
> J.R. Miller

I think Mr. Miller knew the secret, too. Victory is to be won by **sitting first** in God's presence, soaking up His strength and the direction we need. Once full, we can **stand** on His promises and **walk** with confidence in His purposes.

- **Why do you think sitting and waiting is the most difficult?**

Waiting is difficult because we live in a world of **fast**. We have fast food, fast internet, Facebook, Instagram, and email. Do you remember having to wait a week to get film developed? Long gone are the days of 35mm film. Digital downloading is here to stay. But God never changes. He's not going to speed up the waiting process just so that we can get our film developed. He rested, remember? I believe a key component in the waiting is going to the stream **often** during the day. It should be a constant going, a constant flowing, and a constant knowing. Steven Curtis Chapman sings that our "Amen" should never end. It's ongoing and never ending.

LET US PRAY
"And just because we say the word, 'Amen'
It doesn't mean this conversation needs to end. Let us pray, let us pray,
everywhere in every way—Every moment of the day, it is the right time
Let us pray without end and when we finish start again
Like breathing out and breathing in, let us pray."[6]

Reading this makes me want to dive into the river and submerge myself all day long with the Lord. How about you?

• Let's dive into Psalm 40:1.

"I waited PATIENTLY for the Lord and He turned and HEARD my cry."

> "The steps of a GOOD man are ordered by the Lord."
>
> Psalm 37:23
>
> George Mueller wrote in his Bible, "And the STOPS too!" [7]

Waiting is a present participle which means its action is **continuing.** It is used to describe an activity **in progress.** This idea of continuing to wait, leads me to ask these questions: How long did the psalmist wait patiently? How long do **we have to** wait? How long does it take for the Lord to hear our cry? What's our goal anyway? The real question is: **Why do we come to the river?**

We come because we **believe.** We come because we **trust** in the promise that God will turn and hear our cries. When we can't see the plans God has for us, we put our faith and patience in the One who **can** see. God has a purpose, even in the delays. Read the quote by George Mueller. We are made to stop, to sit, to be patient, and to wait with confidence. This **is** where we find our **strength.**

I have a sweet friend named Keisha who heard the Lord after waiting patiently for His direction. When she heard from Him, she moved. Keisha resigned from her job as an assistant school principal and started a ministry for young girls called *The Beauty Within Project.* Waiting is more difficult than walking, but the reward is worth every step. Ask Keisha.

Another key to waiting is not to move without the Lord's direction.

• Why was this important in Exodus 13:21?

_____

_____

• For what have you had to wait? For what are you still waiting? A husband? A job? A baby? A test result? A loss to heal?

_____

_____

One thing is for certain. If we are **focused** on the waiting, we will miss out on the blessings of **TODAY.**

• What do these Scriptures teach us about today?

• Psalm 118:24

_____

_____

• Matthew 6:34

_____

_____

• Matthew 6:27

_____

_____

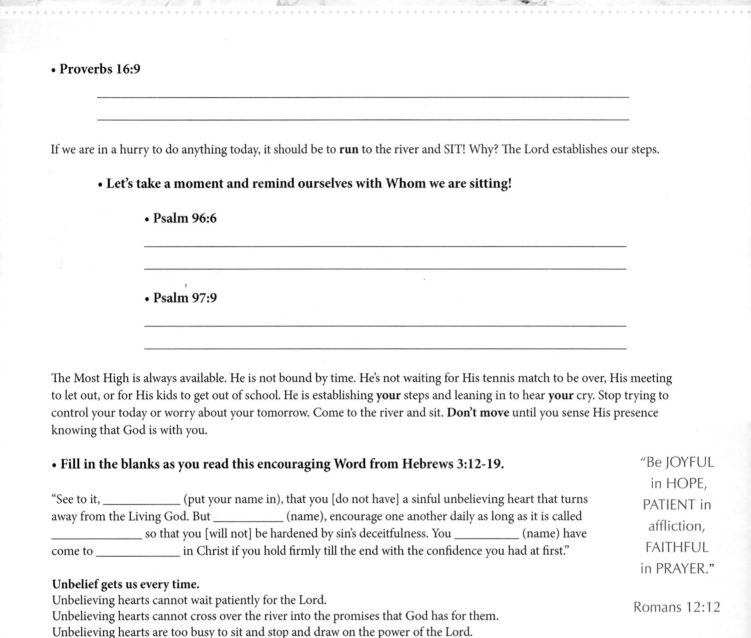

• **Proverbs 16:9**

_____

_____

If we are in a hurry to do anything today, it should be to **run** to the river and SIT! Why? The Lord establishes our steps.

> • **Let's take a moment and remind ourselves with Whom we are sitting!**

>> • **Psalm 96:6**

>> _____

>> _____

>> • **Psalm 97:9**

>> _____

>> _____

The Most High is always available. He is not bound by time. He's not waiting for His tennis match to be over, His meeting to let out, or for His kids to get out of school. He is establishing **your** steps and leaning in to hear **your** cry. Stop trying to control your today or worry about your tomorrow. Come to the river and sit. **Don't move** until you sense His presence knowing that God is with you.

• **Fill in the blanks as you read this encouraging Word from Hebrews 3:12-19.**

"Be JOYFUL in HOPE, PATIENT in affliction, FAITHFUL in PRAYER."

Romans 12:12

"See to it, _____ (put your name in), that you [do not have] a sinful unbelieving heart that turns away from the Living God. But _____ (name), encourage one another daily as long as it is called _____ so that you [will not] be hardened by sin's deceitfulness. You _____ (name) have come to _____ in Christ if you hold firmly till the end with the confidence you had at first."

Unbelief gets us every time.
Unbelieving hearts cannot wait patiently for the Lord.
Unbelieving hearts cannot cross over the river into the promises that God has for them.
Unbelieving hearts are too busy to sit and stop and draw on the power of the Lord.
Unbelieving hearts are deceived and turn away from the Living God.
Unbelieving hearts walk in the counsel of the wicked, stand in the way of sinners, and sit in the seat of mockers.

THE LIVING GOD TURNS US AWAY FROM SIN
SIN TURNS US AWAY FROM THE LIVING GOD

Read the above inset and meditate on this truth for a moment.

Today, O Lord, I pray we choose to sit with You. I pray we choose to wait on You. I pray we choose to trust in You. Turn us away from evil, and fill us to the rim with Your power and strength. You promise us this: "You give POWER to the weak and to those who have no might, You INCREASE their strength" (Isaiah 40:29). Increase our hope when the waiting gets long. Increase our faith when we want to hurry into the appealing promises of an instant society. Help us to believe in You. Help us to focus on Your Word. Help us to be able to come to the river and cross over, leaving our burdens behind. Today is the day YOU HAVE MADE. Let us REJOICE and be glad in it! Amen.

DAY FIVE/ DON'T JUMP THE FENCE

I asked you on the first day to ask yourself **why** you come to the river. My hope is that you have found at least one concrete answer for each day. **Can you name them?**

It's okay. I'm not trying to test you, so I will give you the answers. I wish all tests were this easy!

>   **Day One:** Patience to overlook one's offense.
>
>   **Day Two:** Patience to leave your dirty laundry at the stream and to cross over into God's forgiveness.
>
>   **Day Three:** Patience to be still before the Lord and to wait.
>
>   **Day Four:** Patience to enjoy TODAY and to trust God's leading in everything.
>
>   **Day Five:** Patience to pray and to ALWAYS be thankful.

Today we are going to take a sneak peak into the life of David as he comes to the river.

- **Let's carefully read Psalm 16:1-2, 5-11.**

    - **What is David's first request?**

    _____

    _____

    - **What are the different ways David acknowledges the Lord?**

    I'll start us off:
    You are my LORD. (vs. 2)
    Apart from You, I have no good thing. (vs. 2)
    You have assigned me my cup. (vs. 5)

    _____

    _____

    _____

    _____

David is a picture of our tree—delighting and meditating on the Word of God. He is PLANTED in faith and rooted in love. He rejoices in the safety, refuge, security, counsel, rest, joy, inheritance, and eternal life of the Lord! If you ever get in a pinch and need to be reminded of who God is to you, just read off the promises you have just written down. I am typing so fast right I feel like I am lifting off of my chair in excitement! Who are we that we get to worship this mighty God?

- **What do you think verse 6 means?**

    _____

    _____

    _____

    _____

When we get impatient with God's progress, we are prone to move **beyond** the pleasant boundary lines He has put in place for us.

We had a chicken named Duck. Emphasis on **HAD.** Duck decided one day that she wanted to move beyond the safe boundary lines of our yard and fly over the fence. Duck is now dead. She got enticed by a nice-looking raccoon and was served up for dinner. At the funeral service, my husband gave the kids a memorable eulogy. "Kids," he said with utmost compassion, "God has set your boundary lines in pleasant places. These lines are for your security, rest, and protection. If you choose to go beyond them, you might find yourself plucked, de-feathered, and not coming home anytime soon." Morbid? A bit. True? Right on target.

• **Look at 1 Chronicles 29:11-14.**

"Yours, Lord, is the greatness and the POWER
     and the GLORY and the MAJESTY and the SPLENDOR,
     for EVERYTHING in heaven and earth is YOURS.
Yours, Lord, is the kingdom;
     you are exalted as head over ALL.
Wealth and honor come from you;
     you are the ruler of ALL things.
In your hands are strength and power
     to exalt and give strength to ALL.
Now, our God, we give you THANKS,
     and PRAISE your glorious name.

But who am I, and who are my people, that we should be able to give as generously as this? Everything comes from you, and we have given you only what comes from your hand."

"He will COVER you with His feathers, and under His wings, you WILL find refuge; His FAITHFULNESS will be your shield and your rampart … He will command His angels concerning you to GUARD you in all your ways."

Psalm 91:4,11

This is the foundational verse of my ministry, **ThouArtExalted,**[8] and it is a reminder of the humility we need as we come to the throne of grace. David understood that everything comes from the Lord. Sarah Young writes:

"When you come into My presence, the healing begins. Whether you ask for it or not, My Spirit is at work within your life. But when you come to Me in prayer and ask for My healing, amazing things can happen. Remember that I am a God who can do amazing things—nothing is too difficult for Me"[9]

When we come into the presence of God, He starts working and the healing begins. We do not have to focus on our doubts, worries, or fears, but on God alone and His promises. God loves us beyond and back. He knows what is best for us. He has set perfect boundaries for us within the walls of His Word. And when we come into His presence, the work begins. We can be patient. We can trust when we cannot see the future. We can pray and ask for wisdom and safety. God cares. Let's not wind up on the other side of the fence.

As we close for this week. I want to rewrite Psalm 19 as a personal prayer.

Keep us safe, O Lord—please keep our kids, husbands, friends, and families safe. For ONLY in You do we trust. Goodness knows we live in one crazy world where there is a lot striving for our attention. Thank You for friends that have chosen to love You, too. Keep us from desiring anything that is not of You. Our choice is You first. We are baffled that we are Your choice, too. You have blessed us with so much. Day and night we witness Your loving hand close to us. You've designed our days, and we place our trust in Your plan. Thank You that this life is not the end. Because we believe in Your Son, who conquered death and took our sin, we will live eternally with You. We are planted firmly in Your love and filled with Your joy, because we have sat in Your presence this morning. For this, we are blessed. Amen.

Viewer Guide: Session Four
Believe and Do Not Doubt

We are in our LAST week of sitting! Let's get started.

1. A man's wisdom gives him patience. Patience takes TRUST in God.

> • THREE THINGS happen when we COME and SIT at the RIVER:
> WISDOM, PATIENCE, and TRUST. But we must _____ in God
> and not doubt.

2. WHO is God? Do we really TRUST Him? Do we really believe in who He is?

> *"Much of our addiction to POWER and CONTROL is due to the false conception of who God is."*
> **Timothy Keller:** *Counterfeit Gods*

3. The TREE that is being blessed is giving up the reins of _____. We sit by the river each morning, filling up with the wisdom of the Lord, so we can make good CHOICES.

4. You know when your life is agitated when everyone's name becomes _____.
Who is God to you when life becomes agitated and you are frustrated?

5. Have you ever made a personal decision to believe in Christ? Have you committed your life fully to Jesus?

6. Patience is bearing pain or trials calmly. When trials hit, we have a choice to make. We can either hit the "patience button," or the "_____ button." Do we come to the river with our defenses down?

* 1 Chronicles 28 ~ David's Plans for the Temple

7. King David took the time to SIT and COMMIT his plans to the Lord. David let his defenses down and surrendered his agenda.

"Let your patience show itself perfectly in what you do. Then you will be perfect and complete. You will have everything you need. But if any of you needs wisdom, you should ask God for it. God is generous. He enjoys giving to all people. So God will give you wisdom. But when you ask, you must believe. Do not doubt God."

James 1:4
(ICB)

8. **DO YOUR WORK!**

- Go sit at the river, study the Word, and chew on it! This is HOW God gives us wisdom and patience.

9. God has chosen you to DO a GOOD WORK on this earth, too! God is with you to strengthen you. Do you believe this?

1 Chronicles 29:12-13
"In your hands are strength and power to exalt and give strength to all. Now, our God,
we give you THANKS and PRAISE your glorious name."

10. **Watch me work!** When you surrender your agenda, when you give up control, when you sit with God, you are sitting with the VICTORY and the MAJESTY.

NOTES:

WEEK FIVE: Day One/ A Zillion New Buds

This is our first week to study the **STANDING** portion of **PLANTED**. For the last three weeks, we focused on **SITTING** in the presence of God. That foundation enables us to **STAND** on His promises. During the next three weeks, we will look at **standing** during trials and temptations, **standing** to remember the faithfulness of God, and **standing** on the promises that He … promises.

To STAND means:
- to have or maintain an upright position, supported by one's feet
- to rise to one's feet
- to move to and remain in a specified position[1]

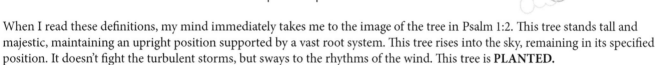

When I read these definitions, my mind immediately takes me to the image of the tree in Psalm 1:2. This tree stands tall and majestic, maintaining an upright position supported by a vast root system. This tree rises into the sky, remaining in its specified position. It doesn't fight the turbulent storms, but sways to the rhythms of the wind. This tree is **PLANTED**.

Today, we will look at two essential truths which allow us to **STAND** during the storms of our lives. The first truth is **standing** on a firm foundation of faith. The second truth is the **process** of **pruning** that keeps us from an unfruitful life. But the question still remains: How do we remain rooted during hardship and still persevere? Do we lift off in a whirlwind of anxiety and fear, or do we remain **PLANTED?** How will these two truths help us? Let's get started on the first one: **STANDING FIRM.**

- **Read Isaiah 7:9. Hopefully this verse will root us again.**

"If you do not STAND FIRM in your faith, you will not STAND at all."

- **In what do you stand firm?**

_____

- **How do you build a strong faith?**

_____

- **If you don't have faith in God, on what do you stand?**

_____

Do you remember the Bible story in which two men built houses on two different foundations? Let's look quickly at Matthew 7:24-29.

- **On what did the wise man build his house?**

_____

_____

- **On what did the foolish man build his house?**

_____

_____

- **What were the outcomes?**

_____

_____

61

Rotten trees fall with a great crash, too. One thing is for certain, trees don't get rotten overnight and neither do we. Did you know a tree can take two years to show signs of decay? I can't help but think we are the same way. We love to look super together on the outside, but on the inside we are slowly dying. Trees die slowly, too. They don't get diseased over the weekend. They take time—just like us. Worry, fear, anger, bitterness, pain, and depression work their way into our root systems—bit by bit. When we have reached our limit where we can't fake our strength anymore, our lives come crashing down. Strong trees are rooted and firmly **planted** to withstand the rain, the rising stream, and the wind beating upon its trunk. Strong women are **PLANTED** firmly in God's Word where faith withstands the doubt, the rising criticism, and the fear of the unknown.

Notice the word again. **Wisdom.**

> "Everyone who hears these words of mine and puts them into practice is like a **wise man** who builds his house on the **rock.**" Matthew 7:24

In her book, *The Altar in the World*, Barbara Brown Taylor says:

> "Wisdom is not gained by knowing what is right.
> Wisdom is gained by PRACTICING what is right." [2]

What did Matthew 7:24-29 say about **practicing**? Let's read it again—"Everyone who hears these words of mine and puts them into practice is like a wise man who builds his house on the rock."

Matthew 7:28 aligns with the passage we studied in week two: James 1:22-25.

We are deceiving ourselves and the strength we perceive we have if we do not **remember** the Word. We must **practice** it by **doing** what it says. We must **STAND** on the firm foundation of our faith and take action if we are to endure the storm. Storms of life test our strength, don't they? They test the foundation of our houses. They test our faith. They test our wisdom. They test **us.** We have to practice what we believe and STAND on the Truth. We have to meet with the Lord at the river to sit with Him and meditate on His Word day and night. Only then, will we be blessed and strengthened to move forward in the storm.

The second truth to STANDING on a firm foundation of faith is the **PROCESS OF PRUNING.**

I've made the conclusion that God prunes trees in one of two ways—an uncontrollable force of nature or an act of mankind. Nature is obviously pruned through the natural forces of wind, disease, blizzards, hurricanes, tornados, and the like. Mankind prunes trees with tools such as chainsaws, clippers, and insecticides. Either way, the tree is pruned from dead limbs, rotten fruit, bugs, or overgrown branches so the tree can **increase in fruitfulness** and grow to its potential.

Not too long ago, my husband and I toured Cumberland Island, Georgia with a naturalist. He explained to us that when fire is caused by a natural source, such as lightning, the Forestry Division does not take immediate action to put out the fire. The fire is nature's way of **pruning** the underbrush and bugs that kill the trees. When controlled, the fire actually **strengthens** the tree because it reduces the overgrowth and the insects that eventually kill it. Amazing really, isn't it? Think about your life. Have you had any hard experiences that pruned the "underbrush" in your life? Can you identify any "bugs" that stunted your growth and fruitfulness in your walk with God? Maybe God has used a storm to **strengthen** you while eliminating jealousy, pride, or anger.

> • **What does Ephesians 4:29-32 tell us we need to prune from our lives?**

_____

_____

_____

"Do not merely listen to the word, and so deceive yourselves. DO what it says. Anyone who listens to the word but does not do what it says is like someone who looks at his face in a mirror and, after looking at himself, goes away and immediately forgets what he looks like. But whoever looks INTENTLY into the perfect law that gives FREEDOM, and continues in it— not forgetting what they have heard, but doing it—they will be BLESSED in what they do."

James 1:22-25

- **When we get rid of these things, in what areas do we find strength?**

_____

_____

> *"...we have COME to SHARE in Christ if we HOLD FIRMLY till the end the CONFIDENCE we had in the beginning."*
>
> Hebrews 3:14

I am convinced God uses both methods of pruning with us as well. He uses **natural circumstances**, ones we cannot control, and He also uses **people** to truthfully detect (in love) those areas in our lives we might need to cut back … or off. One thing is for sure. A tree cannot prune itself. We, too, are not very eager to cut off our rotten limbs. Why? Pruning is neither easy or fun. I remember when I saw Curry prune our rose bushes—correction, HIS rose bushes. I was horrified. They looked terrible. They were bare, scrawny, and pitiful. I was **convinced** they would never recover. But you know what? They did. In fact, the next spring they were **more beautiful**.

God prunes us because He loves us. He can see beyond our buggy lives and into what we will become. He knows what will unfold in the spring. He knows that when we get rid of the underbrush that is prohibiting our growth, we will **stand** stronger in our faith. Two weeks ago, we saw God as the Master Silversmith burning away our impurities and often using the fire of our trials to strengthen us. Today, we see Him as the Master Gardener clipping away the excess. Are you **standing** and trusting in His pruning techniques? Be patient. There are **a zillion new buds** waiting to explode.

Day Two/ A Seed To Sow

Today, we will start with a familiar verse. My prayer is that this passage will take on **new** meaning as we study **STANDING.**

- **Let's open with another verse about the Master Gardener in John 15:1-8.**

  - **Who is the Gardener?**

    _____

    _____

  - **Who is the Vine? What makes this Vine unique?**

    _____

    _____

  - **Who are the branches?**

    _____

    _____

  - **What is the difference between cutting off and pruning the branches?**

    _____

    _____

  - **How do we bear much fruit? What happens when we are apart from the Vine?**

    _____

    _____

Next to this verse, I inscribed these words in my Bible … "The Word of God shapes the will of God in me."
I want us to understand that the time spent **sitting** at the river, filling our root systems (or soul systems) with God's Word, is the time spent **strengthening** our connection to the Vine. When a tree is **PLANTED**, it typically remains or stands there **all** of its life. The soil, water, rain, and sun will feed the small seedling to help it grow into the tree it was meant to be. We, too, are PLANTED.

- **What does John 15:8 say about remaining in the Word?**

_____

_____

God intends that we grow **UP** into the person He created us to be, bearing fruit that will glorify Him, and showing others we are His disciples. The key? **Remaining connected.** Again, this verb is a present participle meaning that it continues to **remain.** It takes daily connection to remain. It takes daily STANDING on the promises of His Word.

- **What does Matthew 13:23 say about this connection?**

_____

_____

The parable of the sower is found in Matthew 13:1-9, 18-23. I know it's a long passage, but it's worth reading. Notice what Jesus does in verse one. I hope this rings a bell by now—hopefully a foghorn. Let's get sowing!

- **Let's break this down to see the verses more clearly. Please fill in the lines.**

    - **Seed scattered on the path. (vs. 4)**
        - **What happened?** _____
        - **What is the meaning? (vs. 19)**_____
        _____

    - **Seed fell on the rocky places. (vs. 5-6)**
        - **What happened?** _____
        - **What is the meaning? (vs. 20-21)** _____
        _____

    - **Seed fell among the thorns. (vs. 7)**
        - **What happened?** _____
        - **What is the meaning? (vs. 22)** _____
        _____

    - **Seed fell on the good soil. (vs. 8)**
        - **What happened?** _____
        - **What is the meaning? (vs. 23)** _____
        _____

- **Let's put some personal application to these verses.**

    - **Can you think of situations in your life when you HEARD the Word of God, but then … ?**

    - You really didn't understand God's Word. You didn't take the time to meditate or delight on it either, so you forgot about it and went on your way?

    - You **did** hear a Word from God, and you were really excited about it! But errands, to-do lists, carpools, meetings, phone calls, work—LIFE got in the way. The Word never even got a chance to take root, so you forgot about it and went on your way.

    - You heard another Word from God and wow, you were jazzed! But that day, your **worries** got the best of you. You felt squeezed by financial obligations, family problems, wanting this and wanting that, window shopping, feeling insignificant and lost. You felt the choke, so you forgot about it and went on your way. (Side note: **choke** actually means to **worry**!)

    - You heard the Word of God. You meditated and delighted on it day and night. You were like a tree **PLANTED** by streams of water. You **stood** on the promises and what happened? You yielded your fruit in season. Your leaf did not wither when the worries of the world tried to choke the promise out of you. You prospered in all you did because the Word was so deeply rooted in you that nothing could snatch it away.

TRUE CONVICTION IS NEEDED
FOR SEEDS TO TAKE ROOT

    - **Can you respond to any of these scenarios?**

    _____

    _____

    _____

    _____

Wow. Do you see the power of being **PLANTED**? Do you see the power of God's blessings when you take the time to **sit** and **stand** on His Word? Yes. We will glorify Him, and people will see that we are His disciples, the sheep of His pasture even when we are persevering during the storm. We will STAND **differently** from the ways of this world because of **how** we handle the storm. **We have true conviction rather than shallow soil.** True conviction is needed for seeds to take root. If we do not take the time to prepare the soil, the Word will not root in our hearts.

Dig into this quote from A. B. Simpson,

"Only by the depth of conviction will our lives amount to anything. Shallow lives live on impulses, impressions, intuitions, instincts, and largely circumstances. Those with profound character look beyond all these and move steadily ahead, seeing the future where sorrow, seeming defeat, and failure will be redeemed. They sail right through the storm cloud into bright sunshine which always awaits on the other side. Once God has deepened us, He can give us His deepest truths, his most profound secrets, and can trust us with greater power. Lord, lead us into the depths of Your life and save us from a shallow existence."[3]

    - **How do you handle trouble and persecution when you are NOT rooted in God's Word?**

    _____

    _____

• How do you handle trouble and persecution when you ARE rooted in God's Word?

_____

_____

Shallow soil will never be enough to satisfy the seed God **plants** in us. You can certainly see where seeds are sown when problems hit your life. Others can too. When we are **not** rooted, we will be uplifted with the first gust of wind. But when we **are** rooted, PLANTED, **standing** on God's Word …

> We are **peaceful** because we are **connected** to the Vine.
>
> We have deep **conviction** because we have **rich soil** to harvest the seed.
>
> We are **confident** because we **know** the Master Gardener personally.
>
> We are **standing** because we **trust** in His promises.

We are examples to others because our lives are proof of the TRUE vine: **Jesus.**

Where are you? Use today as a test of your strength. Whatever happens, imagine your faith growing **deeper.** Cling to the Vine when unforeseen weather whips around the corner. Today, let's sow our seed deep into good soil especially when the worries of the moment and the desire for things try to choke out the Truth. Stand tall. Grow deep. **Grow UP.**

Day Three/ Be Thankful for the Water

How strong did you **stand** yesterday? I know I could have been easily swayed by worry and material wants. As I am writing this study, today is **Black Friday**—the day you **think** you need everything. Come early! Stores open at midnight! Sales only last for the first 100 people! All appliances only five dollars! I can feel the choke already. My sister once told me that you never know what you need until you go shopping. How true. I'm staying home.

> "Seek ye first the kingdom of God and all these things shall be added unto you."
> Matthew 6:33

I will never forget the first time this familiar passage came to life for me personally. Joyce Meyer was in town, and I decided to go alone. This was no easy task. I called in the babysitters, drove downtown, and found a seat to myself among the sea of people. Joyce came out in her matching blue suit, blue shoes, and blue earrings. She said something to this tune, "I could put my value in how I look. After all, I feel so cute in this little outfit. And although God doesn't mind my desire to match or feel good about myself, He wants me to seek **HIM first**—not to focus on the stuff that makes me feel good. God knows my needs. He knows my wants. But He also knows this: If I don't have it, **I obviously don't need it."**

Our family was expecting number three, and we were looking for a bigger house. We set our hearts on **one** in particular. We had placed an offer, invited an architect over to see if we could expand a closet into a nursery, and even prayed in the backyard. The only problem was it needed **lots of work,** and we had maxed out our budget. But, by golly, I was going to **make** it work.

My determination was seen in many "money saving" strategies and most pronounced at our local sandwich shop. My kids and I stopped in to grab a bite to eat. But instead of ordering the usual, I told them they were going to split their sandwiches and be thankful for water, not soda. I was saving already. "Mommy, why can't we have a Coke™?" they questioned. I looked at them square in the eyes and said, "You know, Coke™ may taste better, it may even look better, but it's a little more expensive, and we need to be thankful for the water God has given us." During lunch, as I, too, was craving a Coke™ but "thankfully" drinking water, my phone rang. It was our realtor and best friend who simply told me that our sought out, prayed over house had **sold.** WHAT? But … but … I thought we had first right of refusal … but … but. "Sorry, Annie," came the compassionate voice on the other end of the line.

I held back my disappointment until we got home. The second we drove in the driveway, I burst into tears. My kids were highly confused at this point and asked what was wrong. I looked at them and said, "Mommy wanted a Coke™ today. It tasted better, it looked better, but it was a little more expensive. I need to be thankful for the water that God has given me."

I drove back to the sandwich shop and brought a round of Cokes™ for everyone! Just kidding.

God gives us what we **need**, not necessarily what we **want**.

GOD IS NOT THE AUTHOR OF CONFUSION, BUT OF PEACE

• **Let's look at Jeremiah 17:8.**

"They are like trees PLANTED along a riverbank, with ROOTS that reach deep into the water. Such TREES are not bothered by the heat or worried by long months of drought. Their leaves stay green, and they NEVER stop producing FRUIT."

Jeremiah 17:8 (NLT)

I can't seem to find the part about staying strong when the house you **want** sells to someone else. I am guessing it falls somewhere under the category of not being bothered by heat, or staying green, or failing to produce fruit … even when you feel rotten. I know one thing: God is not the author of confusion, but of **peace** (1 Corinthians 14:33).

• **Let's look at Psalm 23.**

A psalm of David

"The Lord is my shepherd, I shall not be in want.
He makes me lie down in green pastures,
he leads me beside quiet waters,
he restores my soul.
He guides me in paths of righteousness
for his name's sake.
Even though I walk
through the valley of the shadow of death,
I will fear no evil,
for you are with me;
your rod and your staff,
they comfort me.
You prepare a table before me
in the presence of my enemies.
You anoint my head with oil;
my cup overflows.
Surely goodness and love will follow me
all the days of my life,
and I will dwell in the house of the Lord forever."

• **What can you gather from this Psalm as we weave in the theme of being PLANTED and STANDING on the promises of God? Can you identify the images of the Eden relationship?**

_____

_____

The first thing I imagine is that the stream we **sit** by is not only peaceful, but also is still and quiet, like glass. I know shepherds would place rocks upstream just to block the rushing waters so their sheep could drink. When the waters are moving fast, the sheep become scared and **refuse** to drink. When the water is calm, they feel safe and **drink** to their fill.

> • **Can you make a connection between the sheep coming to the river to drink and believers coming to the river to sit? If life is rushing by us, are we prone to sit still and drink?**

_____

_____

_____

God leads us to the riverbank to **sit.** Again, we see the images of an Eden relationship where there is restoration, peace, quiet, and the absence of fear and wants. We come to a place where there is protection, goodness, and love. A place where we can dwell **forever.** The word "dwell" means to **sit.** It also means to **remain.** I hope this jogs your memory back to John 15:4:

> "Remain in me, and I will remain in you. No branch can bear fruit by itself; it must remain in the vine. Neither can you bear fruit unless you remain in me."

When we dwell by the river, we **SIT.** When we sit, we **REMAIN.** When we remain, we **PERSEVERE.** And when we persevere, we **STAND … PLANTED** firmly in the promises of God.

If we are sitting with God by the river, we can count on the fact that He is sitting, too—WITH us and IN us. When we get up to walk through our day, we are **STANDING** with God who fills our every need.

Today, I am thankful for the water God has given me. How about you? What promises are you going to STAND on today?

DAY FOUR/ HOPE IN THE STORM

Seven years ago, our family received a phone call that no one anticipated. The unexpected interruption to an otherwise beautiful day. We were traveling home from Orlando when we heard that my husband's father, Gary Pajcic, had a stroke at the age of 58 and was rushed to the hospital. Three days later, he died from encephalitis, an irritation and inflammation of the brain, most often due to infections. The doctors never could pin the reason for his sudden death. Gary may have been bitten by a mosquito. We will never know.

Gary was not only my father-in-law, but also my brave hero. In Bob Goff's book, *Love Does*, he describes a friend of his who was "secretly incredible, who did not measure his value by what he had but by what he would be willing to give up."[4] Gary was secretly incredible. I have never met a more generous, fun-loving, compassionate, "Love-Does" man. He would help anyone who crossed his path—whether rich, poor, black, white, educated, or non-educated. Gary never gave because he wanted recognition but simply because it was in his DNA. Gary was, to me, *Jesus in disguise.*[5] Coming from a meager background, he excelled in high school both academically and athletically. He was the quarterback for the Florida State Seminoles in the 1960s, went to FSU law school, and began his family and career in Jacksonville. I married his second son.

Hope.

> • **What does your tree look like when the storm hits—unexpectedly?**

_____

_____

_____

_____

- **We looked at Romans 5:3-5 in week three. Today, it's worth revisiting.**

- **Read Romans 5:3-5.**

Was I feeling short changed? Honestly? Yes. Did Gary's death make sense to me? No. Did Gary's death take God by surprise? No. Where was I to go to develop this passionate patience called perseverance? Where was I to go to understand this sudden tragedy? Where was I to go when I felt no hope? I went to the river.

- **Have you felt this way before? Where did you go?**

Romans 5:3 reminds us we are to rejoice in suffering. Why? The suffering we experience produces perseverance, character, and hope. HOPE in the promise that God loves us far beyond our disappointments. HOPE that when we come to **sit**, **stand**, and **walk** with Him, He will pour so much Holy Spirit into our lives that we will be **overflowing**. HOPE in the fact that Jesus died for us, therefore we can confidently climb into His lap and spill out the anguish in our hearts and souls. When the winds blow, our roots have to remain **PLANTED**.

- **What does Scripture say about what to do when the winds start blowing, phones start ringing, and disappointments are at a toxic level?**

    - **1 Chronicles 16:11-12**

    _____

    _____

    - **Psalm 77:11**

    _____

    _____

    - **Psalm 143:1**

    _____

    _____

    - **Deuteronomy 6:4-8**

    _____

    _____

What is the repeated word you hear in these verses? Yes. **REMEMBER**. Remember what the Lord has done! Remember His strength. Remember His miracles. Remember His faithfulness and righteousness. Tell it to your children when you sit, stand, and walk. Why? When we remember, we are filled with **HOPE**.

Let's take a look at two people in the Bible who _remembered_ when they got the unexpected phone call.

- **How did Esther receive the phone call? Read Esther 4:12-16.**

    _____

    _____

"There's MORE to come. We continue to shout our praise even when we're hemmed in with troubles, because we know how troubles can develop passionate patience in us, and how that PATIENCE in turn forges the tempered steel of virtue, keeping us ALERT for whatever God will do next. In ALERT expectancy such as this, we're never left feeling SHORT CHANGED. Quite the contrary—we can't round up enough containers to hold everything God generously pours into our lives through the Holy Spirit!"

Romans 5:3-5
(NLT)

69

• **How did David receive the phone call? Read 1 Samuel 17:34-37.**

_____

_____

_____

Esther **remembered** the faithfulness of God and gathered her people to pray and fast for her while she did the impossible. Going before the King unannounced meant sudden death for Esther unless he extended his golden scepter—even if she was his wife. Esther **stood** on the promises of God when her people, the Jewish nation, had been subject to annihilation. She boldly went before the King, against all odds, and pleaded with him for her people.

David **remembered** the times when the Lord delivered him as he rescued his sheep from bears or lions. In the battle with the Philistines, David stepped out with confidence and **stood** on the promises of God's faithfulness, believing he would once again be delivered as he fought against Goliath.

Where do you need to step out and **STAND** on the faithfulness of God and **remember** His promises? Remember, Jesus is the source of everything we do. We need to rely on His strength and focus on HIM when life throws us a curve ball. We need to be healthy trees that stand tall and firm, **deeply rooted in faith.**

DAY FIVE/ DEEP CALLS TO DEEP

Let's review before we step into day five. Together, we have discussed four days on **standing** with perseverance. **Day one** began with **standing** on the **foundation of faith** and the importance of **pruning** in order for our lives to become more fruitful. **Day two** showed us that we need to **stand** on the **rich soil of conviction** in order for God's Word, the seed, to be deeply planted. Conviction also teaches us to **remain** connected to the Vine because apart from God, we can do nothing. **Day three** walked us back to the riverbank where we **stood** with **thankfulness** because God wants to sit with us, protect us, and guide us to still water. **Day four** taught us that we can **stand** and **remember** the hope that has been offered to us. Jesus is our hope, and He will never disappoint, even when life is disappointing. My hope is that you will remain standing and persevere through the hardships as your strong healthy roots dig deep into your belief and **faith** in the Lord.

Today, I want us to dig even deeper.

• **Let's begin by reading Psalm 42:2, 5-8.**

• **In modern-day terms, what do you think the psalmist could be going through?**

_____

_____

• **What does he do to relieve his downcast heart?**

_____

_____

• **What do you think the phrase "deep calls to deep" means? (verse 7)**

_____

_____

The great 18th century preacher, Charles Spurgeon says this:

> "Remember, our faith is always at its greatest point when we are in the middle of the trial,
> and confidence in the flesh will never endure testing."[6]

When you are in deep sorrow, deep trouble, deep anger, or deep bitterness, where do you go? The psalmist does a number of things that I believe are worth looking into.

First, he recognizes his THIRST for God.

Amid the struggles in life, Spurgeon has it right on the money. Confidence in the flesh will never endure the testing. Finding confidence in friends, spouses, pastors, and parents is not necessarily a bad thing. The truth is, people will eventually fail you. God will not. In the middle of a trial, only a deep confidence in God will satisfy your thirst.

I did a quick study on the effects of trees in drought situations. Texas A&M's Forestry Service concluded that trees normally have a moisture content of 125-200% or more. During prolonged droughts, this percentage can drop below 100% putting the tree in harm. They refer to this water deficit as "water stress." Severe water stress can injure and eventually kill a tree while also making it more prone to forest fire, disease, and insect invasion.[7] Are you making the connection? We, too, have water stress when we are tying to make it on our own efforts and depending on our own flesh. God wants you trust in Him and to drink abundantly from His source. He never promises to take your storm away, but He does promise He will be with you step-by-step and guide you with His Holy Spirit. He promises a **peace** that surpasses human understanding and that **all** things will be beautiful in its own time.

• **Look at Ecclesiastes 3:11.**

> "Yet God has made everything beautiful for its own time. He has PLANTED eternity in the human heart,
> but even so, people cannot see the whole scope of God's work from beginning to end." (NLT)

Did you see the word **PLANTED?** Each life that is born on this earth has the seed of eternity **planted** in their souls. An oak acorn has the DNA of an oak tree from the very beginning. We, like an acorn, have Heaven's DNA placed in each of us. We have been **planted** from the beginning and will grow into **all** that God has created us to be. We naturally crave the Living Water, because whether we can explain it or not, it feeds our souls. We long for the Eden-relationship because **we were born to exist there.**

• **Are you thirsty? Are you drinking from the right source?**

• **Read Psalm 78:12-16.**

• **What did God do with the rocks in the desert and the rocky crag?**

_____

_____

• **Has God provided for you when you thought there was no hope?**

_____

_____

Yes! God provided water, even in the desert. When we are deep in despair, run to His well of Living Water where He provides the water we need for healing and refreshment. In the desert situations of our hardships, God provides abundant water. When our life hits a snag on the rocky crag, God provides streams that flow down like rivers. The psalmist recognized his thirst, not for a temporary water-fountain break, but for the **Living River**. It's the only river that will satisfy our parched souls. We were born to drink from it. We were born to be **PLANTED** by it.

Second, the psalmist puts his hope in the Lord and REMEMBERS His faithfulness (day four's discussion).

Third, his call for the Lord goes DEEP.

Deep calls to Deep.

Have you ever been scuba diving? I remember one day, in particular, heading out for the wide-open seas. Only this day, the seas were not only "wide-open," but the waves were measuring about six feet. White caps were breaking, and I was beginning to have second thoughts when our diving instructor directed us to jump into the water. Following his lead, I jumped right in and immediately became mesmerized by the beauty underneath the water. What really amazed me though, was the **peacefulness under the surface.** On top, it was rough and unstable. Underneath, it was calm and completely undisturbed.

When storms stir the ocean's surface, the bottom remains … **still.** The deep remains **peaceful.** Deep calls to deep. We can be like this, too. When we experience battering circumstances and unforeseen storms, we can dive deep into the depths of peace. We are **rooted.** We can STAND and persevere in trials, because we are **PLANTED.**

Listen to the words from an ancient hymn *Joyful, Joyful, We Adore Thee,* by Henry J. van Dyke, (first and third stanzas).

> "Joyful, joyful, we adore Thee, God of glory, Lord of love;
> Hearts unfold like flowers before Thee, opening to the sun above.
> Melt the clouds of sin and sadness; drive the dark of doubt away;
> Giver of immortal gladness, fill us with the light of day!
>
> Thou art giving and forgiving, ever blessing, ever blessed,
> Wellspring of the joy of living, **ocean depth of happy rest!**
> Thou our Father, Christ our Brother, all who live in love are Thine;
> Teach us how to love each other, lift us to the joy divine."[8]

Oh Lord, teach us how to tap into this joy of living. Teach us how to experience this **ocean depth of happy rest** when we feel that life is a wreck around us. Teach us to recognize our thirst for the Living Water. Teach us how to grow our roots **deep** during the storms of life, to be thankful, and to persevere with faith. Teach us to **remember** Your faithfulness and put our HOPE in You. Teach us to go **deep.**

Teach us to **STAND.**

Father, I pray today that we will stand on Your promises when life is uncertain.
I pray we will be joyful because we adore You! You have planted us with eternity in our hearts,
and we long for the day that we can be in Your presence.
You are the giving and forgiving, and we are ever blessed. Thank You for this week of study.
I pray to persevere in hope and joy
with the strength that You have already provided.
Amen.

Viewer Guide: Session Five
Why we believe what we believe

> "If you do not STAND FIRM in your faith, you will not STAND at all."
>
> Isaiah 7:9

We made it to our FIRST week of standing! Let's get started.

1. The definition of STAND:

    to have an upright position, to rise to one's feet, to REMAIN in a specified position.

2. Are we STANDING on a firm foundation of truth? What is TRUTH?

* TRUTH comes through _____. Jesus is the One and _____. He is God Himself. Jesus is the TRUTH. Do you believe this?

3. We are MORE than conquerors. Paul says, "I am _____." I believe with out a doubt.

"Paul's mind has been persuaded by the truth of who God is, the revelation that ALL of God is in Christ, in the work of Christ. This revelation is the basis of a convinced mind and heart, not an emotional search."
~Alistair Begg, *One Place Podcast*

Paul's mind was convinced that Jesus was and is the TRUTH. We cannot live on an _____ CHRISTIANITY. Our faith has to be BUILT on the solid rock.

4. Paul had to be convinced both in his MIND and in his HEART. The heart is where the _____ begin, but our mind is where we know the FACTS to be true.

5. Satan was a LIAR from the beginning, there is NO TRUTH in him. Jesus is and has always been the TRUTH. Why do we not believe? Satan's number one goal is to _____ us from the TRUTH.

The craftiest tool in Satan's shed is _____.

QUICK "Camp Fire" Review:

- We need to STAND _____ in our conviction of who Jesus is, rather than an emotional Christianity.
- Jesus is the _____. He is God. He is filled with grace and TRUTH.
- Satan is a LIAR and wants nothing less than to fill our minds with _____.

6. How can we know the way? Jesus said, "I am the way, the truth, and the life" (John 14:6). Jesus wants us to TRUST Him.

GO WITH WHAT YOU KNOW! God has PLANTED in us a desire to KNOW Him. He has PLANTED _____ in our hearts (Ecclesiastes 3:11).

- When the seed of God's Word falls on DOUBT, it will not _____. What is choking you?

Sin's deception turns us away from the LIVING GOD,
but the LIVING GOD turns us away from sin.

7. We need to have a **CONFIDENT CONVICTION** to STAND on the promises of God.

Allow Pruning • Remember to Remember • Call on the Deep

* PRUNING makes our faith stronger in God. But we have to prepare the soil. Save us from a SHALLOW EXISTENCE!

* REMEMBER the faithfulness of God. Remember to STAND on the foundation of TRUTH. It is our CHOICE.

* Going DEEP into the TRUTH of God. When troubles come, rest in the stillness of Jesus. We have the OCEAN DEPTH of HAPPY REST. God wants us to LIVE abundantly.

NOTES:

WEEK SIX: DAY ONE/ CHICKEN COOPS AND PARTY KITCHENS

Last week, we concentrated on **STANDING** and persevering during the storms of life. This week, we will look at **STANDING** in the power of the Holy Spirit and allowing our fruit to **yield** in season. We will explore what our "fruit" looks like and how our lives can continue to be fruitful even in times of drought. When we are rooted in the streams of Living Water, we can STAND on the promise that our lives will represent a fruitful tree, no matter the season.

> • **Look up Philippians 2:13 in your own Bible and then read the following translation from the New Living Translation.**

"For God is working in you giving you the desire and power to do what pleases Him."

Read this several times **slowly**. Emphasize each word. For example:

GOD is working in you …
        God **IS** working in you …
                God is **WORKING** in you…

Continue reading this verse and delight in the different ways this passage will speak to you. Rick Warren calls this the **Pronounce it!** Method.[1]

> • **Let's answer these questions together from Philippians 2:13.**

> > • **Who is working in you?**

_____

> > • **What tense is the verb?**

_____

> > • **What is He doing?**

_____

> > • **What is He giving to us that enables us to go through life and bear much fruit? Why?**

_____

_____

_____

I told you the story of Duck's demise when she decided to fly over the boundaries of her chicken coop. After her untimely death, we decided to replace her with three Rhode Island Reds. This meant we needed to buy another chicken coop to house our new little additions.

While searching for a chicken coop, I was experiencing what normal mothers encounter every two months—the **"I-have-got-to-clean-out-our-house-or-else"** feeling. And this time, I was serious. It was time to clean out! And our wooden party kitchen was my target. My children were simply outgrowing the indoor barbecues of plastic hot dogs and pretend ketchup. We all said our "good-byes" and watched Curry load up our beloved party kitchen into the back of my SUV.

I decided from the get-go we were going to find a special home for our party kitchen, perhaps even one we could visit, just so we could all join hands, sing a song or two, and go down memory lane. I called our school. "No, I'm sorry Annie, we already have a party kitchen." I called our church. "No, I'm sorry Annie, we already have a party kitchen." "Okay," I told the Lord, "I am not giving up! I know You have the **perfect place** for our party kitchen. I just know it!"

I pulled up to the *Feed and Seed* and immediately found the perfect chicken coop. While I was at the checkout counter, it dawned on me that I did not have ANY room in my SUV because I had a party kitchen in the trunk. I must have said this out loud because the sweet woman behind the desk said, "You have a party kitchen?" "Y--E--S," I hesitantly said. You see, I didn't want to give away my party kitchen to just anyone. It was our **b-e-l-o-v-e-d, w-o-o-d-e-n** party kitchen. I then learned the sweet woman behind the counter was named Ann. I liked her already! She told me, just that very weekend, she and her mother were at a garage sale looking at a party kitchen for her two-year old little girl. However, the one she found was too expensive. Ann told her Mom that if the party kitchen was still there by the end of the day, she would come back and buy it. It was gone.

This is where GOD, working **in** ME, began to give me the DESIRE and POWER to do what I couldn't do alone.

"Ann," I said, "I want you to have my party kitchen—for free. In fact, I believe God wants you to have our party kitchen."

Her eyes welled up with tears, as did mine. Imagine two grown women crying over a party kitchen in the middle of the *Feed and Seed*. Nonetheless, we unloaded the kitchen and loaded up the chicken coop. Perfect fit.

When you STAND, your Fruit will Bless those around you

Has God ever given you the power to do something that seemed impossible? Have you ever felt compelled to write a letter asking for forgiveness? Have you ever had a hard conversation with a co-worker, spouse, or child? Have you ever had to give up something very precious to you? Tapping into His holy water taps us into the power of His Holy Spirit. This power gives us the strength to do the things we, in and of ourselves, cannot do. When we **STAND** on the promise that the God of the universe is working in us, giving us the power and desire to DO what pleases HIM, He is glorified. And sometimes, He allows us to watch Him work. We get to see first-hand how the fruit of obedience is a blessing to others.

- **Let's close today by looking up some Holy Spirit fruit in Galatians 5:22-23.**

  - **What is the fruit of the Spirit?**

    _____

    _____

  - **What aspect of your fruit do you need today to give you the desire and power to DO what pleases GOD?**

    _____

    _____

When we are **PLANTED** in God's Word, the fruit we bear is a **testimony** to His power and love. God blessed me with the fruit of peace, love, and kindness to give up something. God allowed me to see beyond the temporary and bless Ann with the proof of His love. He also gave me the power of trust to see that I needed to **STAND** on His faithfulness. And when you STAND, your fruit will bless those around you.

In closing, read these wise words from Dr. Charles Stanley.

"We experience His power when we surrender to be used by Him. God releases His power through us as we walk in obedience to Him. One of the ways He releases His power to us is this: Through the fruit of the Spirit, God's power and only God's power enables us to exhibit love, joy, peace, patience, goodness, kindness, faithfulness, gentleness, and self-control, which reveal the character of Christ in us."[2]

Our fruit reveals Christ's character within us. How are you going to share the fruit of your tree with someone today?

Trust.
      Believe.
            STAND.

Who knows? Your gift of a party kitchen could show someone the love of God. **Stand in the power.**

DAY TWO/ THE GIFT THAT KEEPS ON GIVING

Yesterday, I introduced the Holy Spirit's importance in bearing fruit. Before we go any further, let's review our **PLANTED** verse from Psalm 1:1-3.

"Now the earth was formless and empty, darkness was over the surface of the DEEP, and the SPIRIT of God was hovering over the waters."

Genesis 1:2

"Blessed is the one
who does not walk in step with the wicked
or stand in the way that sinners take
or sit in the company of mockers,

but whose delight is in the law of the Lord,
and who meditates on his law day and night.

That person is like a tree planted by streams of water,
which yields its fruit in season
and whose leaf does not wither—
whatever they do prospers."

The first mention of the Holy Spirit is in Genesis 1:2.

- **We learn more about the power of the Holy Spirit in John 14:15-17. Let's take a look.**

- **How does Jesus describe the Holy Spirit?**

_____

_____

- **How can we know the Holy Spirit? Where does He live?**

_____

_____

- **Why can't the world accept the Holy Spirit?**

_____

_____

In the NIV study notes, it states that the Holy Spirit is a counselor and helper that will always **STAND** by Christ's people. I love that.

- **Continue reading John 14:25-27.**

  - **How is the Holy Spirit described here?**

  _____

  _____

  - **Again, we see a contrast with the world. What does Christ offer that is different from the world?**

  _____

  _____

Through our belief in Christ's life, death, and resurrection, we receive the power of the Holy Spirit. With this power comes the promise of a comforter, a counselor, a teacher, and a deep peace. It is a deep sense of rest that all shall be well. This is not the temporary fix that the world offers. This is not an advertisement on Black Friday. This is a decision we make that has **eternal significance**.

- **Look up Ephesians 1:13-14.**

  - **When are we included with Christ?**

  _____

  _____

  - **When we believe in Christ, how are we marked?**

  _____

  _____

  - **What are we guaranteed when we believe in Jesus?**

  _____

  _____

> "Repent, and let every one of you be baptized in the name of Jesus Christ for the remission of sins; and you SHALL RECEIVE the GIFT of the HOLY SPIRIT."
>
> Acts 2:38

The Holy Spirit is proof that we are sealed in Christ. Once we profess He is Lord, we receive this deposit GUARANTEEING what is to come. Just think! The power of the Holy Spirit is just a **down payment**! Remember, we have been **PLANTED** with eternity in our hearts. There is **much** more to come. John 3:16 reminds us that God loved us so much He sent His Son, Jesus, to suffer death for us so we would not perish, but receive eternal life. E-T-E-R-N-A-L life. That's forever! We are just trees passing through this world. It is mind boggling to think of what is to come!

2 Corinthians 5:5 says:

> "Now it is God who has made us for this **very purpose** and has given us the
> **Spirit** as a deposit, guaranteeing what is to come."

God has uniquely fashioned each of us. We are created in His image, and we are called His masterpiece in Ephesians 2:10. I love this Scripture from 1 Corinthians 15:38 in the New Living Translation.

> "A different plant grows from each kind of seed."

"For we are God's MASTERPIECE. He has created us ANEW in Christ Jesus, so we can do the GOOD things he planned for us long ago."

Ephesians 2:10 (NLT)

God shaped you from the beginning. He knew long ago what kind of tree you would become and what fruit you would bear. If you have received Christ, you have the **power** of the Holy Spirit living **inside** YOU. As you bear fruit, you are allowing God to use you to bring others to Him. Your fruit, as we learned in day one, can be love, joy, peace, patience … . When you yield or surrender these qualities to the Holy Spirit, you are bringing **glory** to God. The foundation of **PLANTED** is that YOU are representative of the tree in Psalm 1:2-3. You are blessed with a fruitful life when you are obedient to spend time at the river of Living Water to meditate and delight on God's Word. When you choose to take the time to grow your roots deep, you can't help but bear the fruit God has created in you to produce—even in times of difficulty. The Holy Spirit is the gift that keeps on giving and the fruit that keeps on producing.

Let's allow His Power in us to be a testimony to glorify and bring others to Him.

DAY THREE/ THE FRAGRANCE

Have you ever passed by a fruit tree in the spring? Have you ever stopped and smelled a honeysuckle vine? Oh, the sweet aroma! As fruit trees, we, too, have a smell. Did you know that?

• **Let's read 2 Corinthians 2:14-16.**

    • **To what is the knowledge of Christ compared?**

_____

_____

    • **Who is the one smelling?**

_____

_____

    • **Why is the Christian testimony a "smell of death" to some and a "fragrance of life" to others?**

_____

_____

We smell. To some, we smell good. To others, we smell like the stinky socks I just washed by hand **before** I stuck them in the antibacterial cycle of our washing machine. The *NIV Study Bible* explains it a bit more formally: "The two ultimate categories of mankind are 'those who are being saved and those who are perishing.' To the latter, testifying Christians are the smell of death, not because the gospel message has become evil-smelling or death-dealing, but because in rejecting the life-giving grace of God unbelievers choose death for themselves. To those who welcome the gospel of grace, Christians with their testimony are the fragrance of life."[3] Our fruit bears the aroma of our Christian character.

I have worn the same perfume since college. It is called *Escape* by Calvin Klein. I am sad to say that because it has been discontinued, I have a stash under my bathroom sink. As I am sure it is turning to alcohol as I type, I **am** going to use it until it's gone! Have you ever noticed the longer you wear a certain perfume, the less you are able to smell it? Why is perfume like this? **We** might not be able to smell it, but you can bet others can!

I had a friend once say to me, "Annie, I didn't see you, but I smelled you." I know this sounds kind of creepy, but it's a great analogy. I want to smell like Christ. I want Him to permeate through the pores of my very being. I want to spend as much time with Him at the river as I can. I want my fruit to be plentiful with service, love, and fragrance. But sometimes I can't smell the aroma. I have no idea how the fragrance of my fruit is impacting others. I believe this is God's strategy to keep a cap on my pride. Fill in the blanks with your name. Philippians 2:13 says God is working in _____ giving _____ the desire and power to do what pleases HIM … not _____.

- **What does Ephesians 5:2 say about fragrance?**
  _____
  _____

- **What is Paul saying that we should be?**
  _____
  _____

- **What are the two ways we should live our lives?**
  _____
  _____

I have included my own illustration of a she-tree spraying the fragrance of her fruit into the world. I am sure it is not *Escape*. If it is, I'm gonna ask her where she got it!

Fragrance. Bearing Fruit. Imitating Christ.

OUR FRUIT BEARS THE AROMA
OF OUR CHRISTIAN CHARACTER

ALWAYS leads me in TRIUMPHAL procession ... who ... But THANKS be to God ... the CHRIST and through me spreads everywhere the FRAGRANCE of the KNOWLEDGE of Him ...
2 CORINTHIANS 2:14

Pastor Greg Laurie says:

"Bearing fruit is essentially becoming like Jesus. Spiritual fruit will show itself in our lives as a change in our character and outlook. As we spend time with Jesus and get to know Him better, His thoughts will become our thoughts. His purpose will become our purpose. We will become like Jesus." [4]

Don't you want to become like Jesus? God says we should **imitate** him. How do we do that? We imitate Him by getting to know Him … by the river.

Through the lessons of this study, we have discovered that God has purposefully **PLANTED** each one of us with the seed of His Word. Seeds grow into trees that bear the fruit resembling the original seed. Jesus is the Word. When planted in our hearts, our fruit should resemble the heart of Christ growing in us. We should reflect His glory and radiate His fragrance. How cool is that?

Extra Verses by the Stream:

• **Let's look at Exodus 29:18.**

• **What kind of fragrance was this offering to the Lord?**

_____

_____

This offering was a sin offering for the past sins of Aaron and his sons. They burned the ram before the Lord, and the sins were transferred to this unblemished ram. The ram became the sin-bearer, and God was satisfied with the aroma of their sacrifice.

• **What does the end of Ephesians 5:2 say about Jesus?**

"…Christ loved us and gave himself up for us as a fragrant offering and sacrifice to God."

"…fix our eyes on Jesus, the AUTHOR and perfecter of our FAITH, who for the JOY set before him endured the cross, scorning its shame, and SAT down at the right hand of the throne of God. Consider him who endured such opposition from sinful men, so that you will not grow weary and lose HEART."
Hebrews 12:2-3

Jesus gave himself up for us as a **fragrant offering** and sacrifice to God. Do you see the parallel? Only Jesus' sacrifice and His suffering for our eternal salvation is a holy fragrance that is **permanent.** It never loses its fragrance. It's a sealed deal.

Read the words of Austin Phelps.

"Suffering is a wonderful fertilizer for the roots of our character. The great objective of this life is character, for it is the only thing we can carry with us into eternity. And gaining as much of the highest character possible is the purpose of our trials." [5]

We are called to **imitate Christ**. Suffering is a guaranteed part of our character development and our pleasing fragrance. It's the suffering that **builds** our character. Have you ever smelled a pine log that is burning? The aroma is pleasing. I am not implying that God wants us to go through trials so He can smell some pine kindling. I am saying our trials mold us into the tree we need to become. When we **STAND** on the promises of God, not bending to the ways of the world, we **are** the fragrance of Christ. Our trials are a fragrant aroma to the Lord because we are **standing firm.**

Read Hebrews 12:2-3 in the left-hand margin. Are you going to smell like Jesus today? Imitating Jesus is a lot easier when the sun is shining, your car is clean, your bed is made, and everyone is getting along. What about the harder days when an argument breaks out, the test results come back, the report cards come in, or the check does not arrive. How will you smell that day? Let's roll around in some **holy fertilizer.** Let's not grow weary and lose heart. Let's yield our fruit in season. Let's build our character to imitate Jesus and smell like Him, too.

DAY FOUR/ REAL CARNATIONS

Are you ready for a day with **PLANTED** imagery in just about every verse? Let's **STAND** on one of the first instructions God gave to man.

> • **Read Genesis 1:28**.
>
> "And God blessed them, and God said unto them, Be fruitful, and multiply … "

What is the first thing God does with man? Remember our key verse? "Blessed is the man who … ." God is in the business of **blessing**. What does God tell them next? Yes! Be fruitful and multiply. If I looked at you today and said, "Katie, be fruitful!" Would you have any clue what I was trying to say? Probably not. Let's examine what being fruitful really means.

Being fruitful, as you would expect, is: "to bear fruit, to cause to bear fruit, or to show fruitfulness." [6]

> • **We saw the word fruitful in a passage we studied last week. Let's take another look at John 15:1-8. How many times do you see the word fruit in this passage?** _____

Digging a little deeper …

> • **What is implied about the fruit in John 15:2?**
> _____
> _____
>
> • **What is implied about the fruit in John 15:4?**
> _____
> _____
>
> • **What is implied about the fruit in John 15:5?**
> _____
> _____
>
> • **What is implied about the fruit in John 15:8?**
> _____
> _____

Let's look up FOUR ways we can yield our fruit in season:

FIRST: God prunes us (our discussion in week five). He does this not because we are bad fruit trees, but because He knows the cutting back of bad branches will only make us **more** fruitful. The man who walks, stands, and sits with the wicked is not fruitful in the least. The man who is remaining in the Vine will yield fruit in season.

> • **Read Proverbs 12:3.**
>
> "A man cannot be established through wickedness, but the righteous cannot be uprooted."

We cannot be established through wickedness. Never. But one thing is for certain, when we are attached to the Vine, we will never be uprooted!

SECOND: We cannot bear fruit on our own even when we try really hard!

> • **Read Proverbs 11:28.**
>
> "Whoever trusts in his riches will fall, but the righteous will thrive like a green leaf."

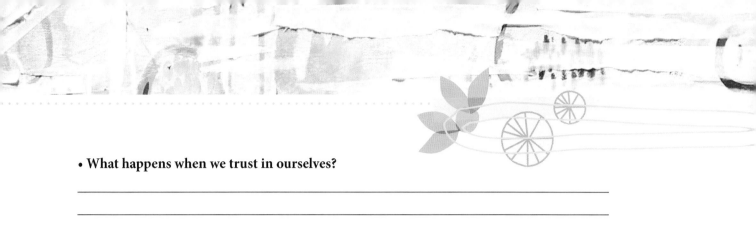

- **What happens when we trust in ourselves?**

_____

_____

- **What happens when we trust in the Lord?**

_____

_____

"As the RAIN and the SNOW come down from HEAVEN, and do not return to it without WATERING the earth and making it BUD and flourish, so that it yields SEED for the SOWER and bread for the eater, so is my WORD that goes out from my mouth: It will NOT return to me empty, but WILL accomplish what I DESIRE and ACHIEVE the PURPOSE for which I sent it. You will go out in joy and be led forth in peace; the mountains and hills will burst into SONG before you, and ALL the TREES of the field will clap their hands."

Isaiah 55:10-12

I am not a green thumb, but I do know when plants are thriving and when they are not. I want to be a green leaf. How about you?

- **Read Isaiah 55:10-12.**

- **Who waters our tree so we can be this green leaf and bear the fruit?**

_____

_____

As we have discussed, God has planted us all unique from the beginning. We are all different trees bearing different fruit. But we do have one thing in common—the Word of God. We see here, in a beautifully poetic way, that as the rain from Heaven waters the earth, the Word of God waters our souls. When God's Word is spoken, it has power and purpose. It yields seed for the sower to bud and flourish. When we receive the seed, we will be filled with JOY and will be led out in peace. When we try to bear fruit on our own, it will always turn sour. When we allow God's rain to fall into our lives and to grow the seed in us, even the trees will rejoice and clap their hands! Of course, they will! Don't you love the imagery? I might be under the "tree spell" right now, but I am beginning to see people as trees. I will look at a huge oak with outstretched limbs and say, "That looks like Mother Teresa." I will look at a beautiful blooming orange tree and say, "That one looks like Nancy. There is so much knowledge and wisdom on that tree." A colorful crepe myrtle reminds me of my best friend growing up—Dearing, who has so much personality and flair. Then you drive by the half-dead ones. You can put personalities on those, too. Just don't mention the names in your small group! What kind of tree are you? Try putting personalities to the trees. It's rather fun!

THIRD: We have to remain at the riverbank if we want to bear the fruit that glorifies the Lord. We can **stand** on the promise that when we remain in Him, we WILL bear much fruit.

STAND on this promise from Philippians 1:6.

"There has never been the slightest doubt in my mind that the God who started this great work in you would keep at it and bring it to a flourishing finish on the very day Christ Jesus appears." (MSG)

God is continually working in us, and we can **stand** on the promise that He will carry the work He has created for us to do, our fruit, until completion.

83

FOURTH: Bearing fruit is ALL to His glory … not ours.

> • **Read Proverbs 11:30.**
>
>> "The fruit of the righteous is a tree of life, and the one who is wise saves lives."

Are you a fruitful tree? When we are **PLANTED** firmly in the Word of God, our fruit is bearing life for others. We are the aroma of life. We are the aroma of Christ.

Let's close today by reading Galatians 6: 7-8, from *The Message.*

> "Don't be misled: No one makes a fool of God. What a person plants, he will harvest.
> The person who plants selfishness, ignoring the needs of others—ignoring God!—harvests a crop of weeds.
> All he'll have to show for his life is weeds! But the one who plants in response to God, letting God's
> Spirit do the growth work in him, harvests a crop of real life, eternal life."

Have you ever seen the science experiment with a white carnation and blue food coloring? When you place the carnation in blue water, it turns blue! We are the same way. If we plant ourselves in the ways of this world, we are going to absorb worldly character. If we plant ourselves by the streams of Living Water, we are going to absorb godly character. We reap what we sow. Our fruit is **proof** of where we are planted. Again, we see the contrast between Psalm 1:1 and Psalm 1:2-3. We will not be blessed if we stand in the way of sinners and plant ourselves to please our own selfish desires. We will be blessed if we are PLANTED with the power of the Holy Spirit. This tree, this woman, who sows the Word of God will reap the Spirit of life— eternal life. She is bearing the fruit that spreads the fragrance. Let's be a real carnation today and not be filled with the dye of this world.

DAY FIVE/ A TREE IS KNOWN BY ITS FRUIT

The past four days, we have looked at the meaning of being **fruitful**. We have discussed the power of the Holy Spirit in giving us the desire to bear spiritual fruit. We have also looked at bearing fruit that smells like Christ and glorifying God in the fruit of our service to others.

> • **What do these three passages tell us about fruit?**
>
>> • **Proverbs 12:14**
>>
>> _____
>>
>> • **Proverbs 18:20**
>>
>> _____
>>
>> • **Matthew 12:33-35**
>>
>> _____

> • **What do these three passages have in common?**
>
> _____
>
> _____

From the **fruit** of his lips a man is filled with good things as surely as the work of his hands reward him. From the fruit of his mouth a man's stomach is filled, and with the harvest from his lips he is satisfied.

We could spend **days** on the different aspects of fruit we bear. Today, I want to end this week with two very important ones: Our **speech** and our **heart**. In the context of the Matthew passage, Jesus has just healed a demon-possessed man that was both blind and mute. When the word on the street begins to spread that Jesus could be the son of David, the Pharisees (the Jewish leaders) say this:

> "It is only by Beelzebub, the prince of demons, that this fellow drives out demons. Jesus knew their thoughts and said to them … . 'Make a good **tree** and its fruit will be good, or make a bad **tree** and its fruit will be bad, for the tree is recognized by its fruit. You brood of vipers (talking about the Pharisees), how can you who are evil say anything good? **For out of the overflow of the heart the mouth speaks.** The good man brings good things out of the good stored up in him, and the evil man brings evil things out of the evil stored up in him.'" Matthew 12:33-35

> "A TREE is KNOWN by its FRUIT… Out of the ABUNDANCE of the HEART the MOUTH speaks. A GOOD man out of the GOOD TREASURE of his HEART brings forth GOOD things, and an evil man out of the evil treasure brings forth evil things."
>
> Matthew 12:33-35

Jesus uses the analogy of a **tree** to describe the human race.

My question for you is this: What are you **PLANTING** in your **heart**? Jesus made it very clear that if we plant evil in our heart, we will reap evil. If we sow gossip in our hearts, we will we reap gossip. What about anger, bitterness, or jealousy? We will be recognized by our fruit, and it starts with the heart. Why? Because our hearts are the very core of our souls.

Proverbs 4:23 says:

> "Watch over your heart with all diligence,
> For from it flow the springs of life." (NASB)

The NIV says to **guard** your heart. The idea of "guarding" is that of a watchman keeping guard. He is constantly on the lookout for danger and will go to extreme measures to protect whatever it is he is protecting from harm. In our case, God is telling us to take seriously the constant watch over our hearts. Why? He knows our heart is the hub of our souls. Our heart is the wellspring of life, for from it flows the springs of life! The lexicon meaning of **flowing** represents a place from which any person goes **forth.** When we come to sit by the spring of LIVING WATER each day, we are filling up our hearts with the LIVING WORD going **forth** into the world and **bearing** the fruit of our speech to glorify the LORD. The fruit of our speech reflects the condition of our heart—good or bad. When we spend time at the river, filling our hearts with the goodness of God, we are protecting our hearts because we are being filled with the treasures of God verses the things of this world. Wow.

How are you going to speak today? Matthew tells us our fruit is linked to our words. Each time we speak, we should be **PLANTING** seeds that grow in others' hearts, too. Are your words bearing good seeds?

As we close for the week, think of the trees in your life that have planted **YOU** with the seeds of Jesus. Why not consider writing them a letter telling them how much their fruit has meant to you. Just for fun, think of the tree of which they remind you. Then, draw it in the margin. Just kidding!

VIEWER GUIDE: SESSION SIX
THE INCREDIBLE EXCHANGE

Today we will look at Ephesians 2:10. We are created with a purpose, and God has a plan for each of us.

1. Why did God plant you on this earth?

> **Ephesians 2:10**
> *"For we are God's _____, created in Christ Jesus to do good works,*
> *which God prepared in advance for us to do"*

> "For we are God's MASTERPIECE. He has created us ANEW in Christ Jesus, so we can do the GOOD things he planned for us long ago."
>
> Ephesians 2:10 (NLT)

2. There are **three qualities** about this Ephesians verse:

    1. We are His _____.
    2. We have been created _____ in Christ.
    3. God has a _____ and a plan for us.

* WE ARE HIS MASTERPIECE.

3. We are created in God's _____. We are shaped in His image. Masterpiece can also mean: POIEMA. This sounds like the word _____. We are His poem, and each day we are living out a stanza of His poem. When others read our poem, they see the reflection of _____ in us.

* WE ARE CREATED ANEW IN CHRIST.

4. God made us _____ in Christ. We can do NOTHING to earn our salvation. It is a GIFT. It is through _____ we have been saved through FAITH (Ephesians 2:4-10).

5. We are a new creation! We are Christ's _____ (2 Corinthians 5:17-21). The idea of reconciling is the idea of _____. God exchanged our sinful life for the perfect life of Christ.

* WE HAVE BEEN GIVEN A GOOD WORK TO DO ON THIS EARTH.

5. God is going to do GREAT things through us! We are God's official representatives. This is a high calling! But we are not asked to do this alone. We have the _____ _____, and we will be equipped to do what God wants us to do. It's a promise.

6. John 14:16-17 reminds us the Holy Spirit is our _____, is with us forever, and is the Spirit of _____. He lives in us. He is with us. He _____ us ALL things, and is working IN us.

7. We are a tree PLANTED. The fruit of the RIGHTEOUS is a TREE of _____(Proverbs 11:30). What fruit are you bearing?

* OUR FRUIT REPRESENTS THREE THINGS: *OUR SPIRIT, OUR SPEECH, AND OUR SHAPE*

8. **OUR SPIRIT:** The Fruit of the Spirit is ONE piece of fruit! We have to _____ to God's Spirit to be used by Him.

9. **OUR SPEECH:** Our speech is our fragrance. Our speech is like a seed PLANTED into the hearts of others. It bears the power of life to whom we speak. Spray, Spray, Spray!

10. **OUR SHAPE:** God has given us an assignment. This assignment is not about us but about _____ (1 Corinthians 12:7).

"Stand at the intersection of your affections and successes and find your uniqueness."
~ **Max Lucado,** *The Cure for the Common Life*

Will Jesus see our FRUIT? The deeper you go with GOD, the MORE you become like CHRIST. Amen.

NOTES:

Key to Lesson: Masterpiece, Anew, Purpose, Image, Poem, Christ, Anew, Grace, Ambassador, Exchanging, Holy Spirit, Counselor, Truth, Teaches, Life, Yield, God

Video sessions are available for download at www.thouartexalted.com/PLANTED ~ teaching videos

For our last week of **STANDING**, we will study five different trees in Scripture that are a picture of strength, righteousness, flexibility, blessing, faith, and beauty. We will look at the flexibility of the limber pine and the righteousness of the oak tree. We will see the cedar tree as a symbol of patient faith, the palm tree as a symbol of victory, and the olive tree as the lamp of oil burning to illuminate our Christian faith. As you can imagine, there are **many** references to trees in Scripture, so we will not be able to cover ALL of the information about them. Our focus will be to look specifically at how our Christian life, symbolized by a tree in Psalm 1:3, reflects **STANDING** in faith in Christ. Because Scripture does not tell us the kind of tree that is represented in our PLANTED passage, I believe we have creative license to decide which tree to which God might be referring. Let's get started.

This past summer in Wyoming, I was introduced to a tree called **the limber pine.** Although the limber pine is not specifically mentioned in the Bible (even though pine trees are), I think it's worth a day of study to consider how this tree represents us in so many ways.

The limber pine grows in the western part of the United States and is known for its ability to bend without breaking. Its scientific name is the *pinus flexilis.* I am not a latin expert nor a "treeologist," but I can look at the word **flexilis** and know that this tree must be really flexible!

The limber pine I stumbled upon lives on the Medicine Bow Range in the southern part of Wyoming. This tree not only endures the heat of the summer, but also the cold and ice of the winters. The limber pine adapts to survive the extremes of various weather conditions. In other words, the limber pine **STANDS** in the storm.

> • **Read Psalm 37:3-9. What is God calling you to do as you STAND in your faith? I found ten actions. I'll start you off:**
>
> **Trust …**
> **Do good …**
> **Dwell …**
> **Enjoy …**

_____

_____

_____

> "DELIGHT yourself in the LORD and he WILL GIVE YOU the DESIRES of your heart. Commit your way to the LORD; TRUST in him and he will do this: He will make your RIGHTEOUSNESS shine like the dawn, the justice of your cause like the noonday sun. Be STILL before the LORD and wait PATIENTLY for him; do not fret when men succeed in their ways, when they carry out their wicked schemes."
>
> Psalm 37:4-7

Notice the word **DELIGHT** in verse 4. We also see the word delight in our foundational passage: "Blessed in the man who *delights* in the law of the Lord" (Psalm 1:2). From Psalm 37:4, what is God giving us when we take delight in Him? Yes, He gives us the desires of our hearts. Did you know the word **delight** can mean to soften, to bend, or to be flexible? The Hebrew word is *anag,* meaning: "to make oneself moldable and pliable."[1] God uses our joys, trials, and gifts to **mold us** into the children He has intended for us to be. We also know from John 15 that when we remain attached to the Vine, we will bear much fruit. Apart from God, we become brittle and break off. Now, we see that if we remain bendable and **delight** to His way, God will give, or **plant** in us, the desires of our hearts. The word "give" in Hebrew is *nathan,* meaning: "to ascribe, to entrust, to add, or to write."[2] God is entrusting and writing on our hearts His desires when we come to the river to sit, stand, and walk in His purposes.

When we take the meaning of this verse and parallel it to the imagery of the limber pine, we see that God wants us to be like this tree, planted by streams of water. Just as the limber pine bends to the natural forces of nature, God wants us to bend to His will as well. This is not always easy—especially living in a culture of "have it your own way."

While walking with a friend of mine, I told her about the flexibility of the limber pine. She immediately thought of our tendency to become legalistic and "stiff-necked." She pointed out that when we are not flexible to delight in God's plan our "limbs" can often snap off and hurt others. There have been times my words and actions have hurt people because I was not delighting in the Lord—allowing His will to mold me. Ouch!

- **Can you describe a time when you did not bend to the Lord's desire and your limbs broke off and hurt someone … or even yourself?**

On the flip side, can you think of a time when you were **willing** to bend to the ways of the Lord—trusting that His plan was better than yours?

Psalm 20:7-8 says:

> "Some trust in chariots and some in horses, but we **trust** in the name of the LORD our God.
> They are brought to their knees and fall, but we rise up and **STAND** firm!"

When we trust in our own strength, we can guarantee our branches are going to crack and break. But when we are pliable enough to **TRUST** in the NAME of the LORD, and bend to His will, we will **STAND** strong—just like the limber pine.

- **Look up this passage in 1 Corinthians 15:58.**

"Therefore, my dear brothers and sisters, STAND FIRM. Let NOTHING move you. ALWAYS give yourselves FULLY to the work of the Lord, because you KNOW that your labor in the Lord is not in vain."

1 Corinthians 15:58

- **Why should you stand firm?**

  _____

  _____

- **What tends to "move you" in your relationship with the Lord?**

  _____

  _____

- **How can you give yourself FULLY to the work of the Lord?**

  _____

  _____

When we remain in the Vine and take delight in the Lord with our actions, our service will never be considered an empty activity.[3] Our faith **is** our foundation, and our work **is** for the LORD. It is never in vain. **Never.** Our study this week will take us through the many characteristics of trees found in the Bible. We will also see that as we are flexible to the Lord's will, we will take a **STAND** in our faith. We will seek to answer the questions of **why we stand, how we stand, and for whom we stand.**

- **Look up Psalm 119:71-77.**

  - **Why was it considered good for this Psalmist to experience suffering? (verse 71) What was precious to this person?**

    _____

    _____

  - **What did the Psalmist REMEMBER? (verses 73, 75)**

    _____

    _____

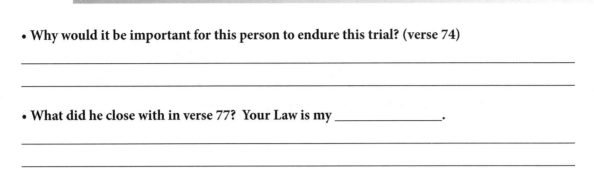

- **Why would it be important for this person to endure this trial? (verse 74)**

_____

_____

- **What did he close with in verse 77? Your Law is my _____.**

_____

_____

As I was studying this passage, I wrote these words in my journal:

> *Lord, when I come to sit at the river, I am amazed that, as I take delight in You, You are just as excited to take delight in me. To delight can also mean to "bend down." I love this idea because I imagine You are bending down to fill me with the joy and desire to serve You more. And in Your presence, I am being molded to Your plan and to Your purposes. I pray today, as I delight in Your Word, I would limber up to Your ways. I pray to be pliable to Your direction, to Your counsel, and to Your wisdom. Amen.*

Not even two hours later, I received an email that changed the entire direction of my ministry. As I thought it was headed in one direction, God took me by complete surprise and closed a door I thought was wide-open. Have you ever played the game *Chutes and Ladders?* This email was similar to the last slide in the game. Just when you **think** you "have it in the bag," you hit the last "chute" that takes you ALL THE WAY back to the beginning. I was at square one. The next day, this is what my journal read:

> *You, Oh Lord, have not led me this far to let me go. Just when I thought my direction was so clear, You closed a door right on my nose. Thanks—It's gonna take a while to recover. But, I know Your plans are good, and You have all the details worked out. My gifts are a fragrance to You, and I pray my life and my ministry will only bring glory to Your Kingdom. I pray to always remain limber enough to be pliable to Your direction and BRAVE enough to press on with Your grace.*

Psalm 119:71 reminds us that the purpose of our afflictions and trials is to draw us closer to the Lord. When we are limber enough to recognize that trials are meant to steer us into God's purposes, others will notice, too.

In closing, notice what Isaiah 55:11-13 says about the pine tree:

> "… so is my word that goes out from my mouth: It will not return to me empty, but will accomplish what I desire and achieve the purpose for which I sent it. You will go out in joy and be led forth in peace; the mountains and hills will burst into song before you, and **all the trees of the field will clap their hands.** Instead of the thorn bush will grow the **pine tree,** and instead of briers the myrtle will grow. This will be for the Lord's renown, for an everlasting sign, which will not be destroyed."

How can a tree clap its hands if it is not limber? Trees are for God's glory, an everlasting sign! Let's rejoice today, go out in peace, clap your hands, and be limber enough to celebrate God's plan … whatever it may be.

Today, write a prayer asking God to make you more limber. You never know, you might be in line for the next game of *Chutes and Ladders*. Remember though, it's not whether you win or lose, but **how** you play the game. I want to play by the Lord's rules, **standing** with Him at my side.

How about you?

"It was GOOD for me to be afflicted so that I might learn your decrees. The law from your mouth is more precious to me than thousands of pieces of silver and gold. Your hands made me and formed me; give me understanding to LEARN Your commands. May those who fear You REJOICE when they see me, … . Let Your compassion come to me that I may live, for Your law is my DELIGHT."

Psalm 119: 71-75

DAY TWO/ THE OAK TREE

Our closing prayer yesterday is the perfect segue into today's lesson about the **oak tree**—the tree also known as the **oak of righteousness** in Isaiah 61.

Oak trees remind me of home. As I look out my office window, the oaks in our yard stand tall and majestic above the colorful azaleas. Oak trees are usually more broad than tall and maintain a low center of gravity which make them hard to blow over. Their limbs are usually close to the ground, providing the perfect jungle gym for any child. Their wood is dense which also makes them very **STRONG.**

Growing up, my father told me the story of "**Old Ironsides.**" During the war of 1812, the U.S. Navy frigate *Constitution* defeated the British frigate, *Guerriere*, in a heated battle off the coast of Nova Scotia. *Constitution* became famous when "witnesses claimed the British shot merely bounced off *Constitution's* side as if the ship were made of iron rather than wood." [4] The ship was 21 inches thick, built from the good ole' oak tree.

In Scripture, the oak is mentioned several times. It is used to describe strong and powerful men in Amos 2:9. The oak tree at Shechem is the site where Jacob buries the foreign gods of his people (Gen. 35:4). In addition, Joshua erects a stone under an oak tree as the first covenant of the Lord (Josh. 24:25-27). In the book of Judges, the angel of the Lord sits under the oak tree and finds rest. In Isaiah 61, the prophet refers to the Israelites as "oaks of righteousness." This is where we will anchor our study for today.

"The Spirit of the Sovereign Lord is on me, because the LORD has anointed ME to proclaim GOOD news to the poor. He has sent me to BIND up the brokenhearted, to proclaim FREEDOM for the captives and release from darkness for the prisoners and a garment of PRAISE instead of a spirit of despair. They will be called oaks of righteousness, a PLANTING of the Lord for the display of His SPLENDOR."

Isaiah 61:1-3

- **Let's begin by looking up Isaiah 61:1-3.**

    - **Who do you think the Spirit of the Lord is anointing to proclaim good news, to bind up the broken-hearted, and proclaim freedom?**

If you answered Christ, you are right! In Luke 4:16-21, Jesus begins his ministry in Nazareth by reading this very Scripture in the synagogue. While all eyes were fastened on Him, Jesus says, "Today this Scripture is fulfilled in your hearing." Jesus is the fulfillment of this Old Testament passage. His earthly ministry proclaimed freedom and liberty for all who believe in His name. Not only does Jesus provide comfort, new life, and beauty, but He also calls believers "oaks of righteousness," a planting of the Lord for the display of His splendor. Although many scholars believe this passage is specifically pointing to the future regeneration of the nation of Israel, I believe we can use this imagery of the strong oak to point to the fact that God is growing us to **STAND tall** and firm, to be a PLANTING for the display of His splendor.

As we have studied **PLANTED** (sitting in the presence of God, standing on His promises, and walking in His purposes), we have compared our Christian life with that of the tree in Psalm 1:1-3. As believers in Christ, we stand **righteous** and **strong** before God. We are **PLANTED** with the purpose of being a symbol of this tree.

- **Let's read Romans 3:21-23 and look at righteousness.**

    - **How does this verse define righteousness?**

      _____

      _____

    - **How do we become righteous according to this verse?**

      _____

      _____

The only way we can become righteous is by believing in Jesus Christ. Righteousness is also a part of the fruit we bear.

> **• What does Philippians 1:9-11 say about bearing the FRUIT of righteousness?**
>
> _____
>
> _____
>
> _____

The New Living Translation refers to fruit as the "fruit of (our) salvation—the **righteous character** produced in our life by Jesus Christ—for this will bring much glory and praise to God" (Philippians 1:11). When we are right before God, we are living for the glory and praise of Him. In addition, He is **continually filling** us with godly fruit when we are PLANTED—sitting, standing, and walking with Jesus.

Not only does the oak remind us that we are a display for His splendor, but also that we are **STRONG** trees when we **STAND** firm in our faith.

1 Corinthians 16:13 reminds us of this:

> "Be on your guard; stand **FIRM** in your faith; be men of courage; be strong."

When we place our trust in God, we rise up and **stand firm** before Him, just like the mighty oak. In Ephesians 6, Paul talks about this while putting on the armor of God.

• Let's read together Ephesians 6:10-18.

> **• How many times does Paul mention the word STAND?**
>
> _____

> **• What part of the body does the breastplate of righteousness cover?**
>
> _____

> **• Why do you think it's so important to protect our hearts against the schemes of the devil?**
>
> _____
>
> _____

"And this is my prayer: that your LOVE may abound more and more in knowledge and depth of insight, so that you may be able to discern what is BEST and may be PURE and blameless for the day of Christ, FILLED with the FRUIT of RIGHTEOUSNESS that comes through Jesus Christ—to the glory and praise of GOD."

Philippians 1:9-11

The heart is the **central station** of our belief. When we receive Christ, we believe in Him by confessing with our mouths and accepting Him in our hearts (Romans 10:10). Once we accept Jesus, we are sealed with the power of the Holy Spirit. Still, our hearts can get us into trouble. Therefore, we need to protect it with the "belt of Truth," which is God's Word. Just as the mighty oak tree endures the battle of natural forces and remains strong, we, too, are called to put on the full armor of God and **stand** our ground when the day of evil comes. The oak is a constant reminder for us to guard our faith and our hearts when life hits unforeseen climates.

The oak is the symbol of **our strength and righteousness** in the Lord. It is also a symbol of **PRAISE.** The oak's tree limbs are lifted HIGH in all of God's glory. We, too, lift our hands and praise Him for all that He is, all that He has done, and ALL that He will do. Let's close today by reading Psalm 63:2-5. When you read this verse, lift your hands up high and place a picture of the beautiful oak tree in your mind.

"O God, you are my God;
I earnestly search for you.
My soul thirsts for you;
my whole body longs for you
in this parched and weary land
where there is no water.
I have seen you in your sanctuary
and gazed upon your power and glory.
Your unfailing love is better than life itself;
how I praise you!
I will praise you as long as I live,
lifting up my hands to you in prayer.
You satisfy me more than the richest feast.
I will praise you with songs of joy."

Psalm 63:1-5 (NLT)

Let's lift our hands in praise because we worship a **mighty God!**

DAY THREE/ THE CEDAR TREE

Today, as we look at the **cedar tree**, we will also "cross pollinate" and touch on the palm tree.

I am so intrigued by the idea that we are considered trees PLANTED by streams of water. I hope that you are, too! You may even want to get a highlighter and mark some of the **main** facts about the trees we are studying. This way, you can visualize the similarities between trees and our Christian faith. I am not saying that we will grow bark, live over 200 years, or repel worms, but we CAN gain insight into the strength, purpose, and fruit from which these trees are PLANTED.

The **cedar tree** is another majestic tree that has significance in Scripture. The cedar is known for its height, girth, and lifespan. It can reach over 120 feet tall, 40 feet wide, and live more than 2,000 years! Its wood is full of resin that preserves it from rot, as well as worms and insects. The wood is hard, free from knots, and is close-grained, which makes it good for building. Cedar trees were used to build many things in the Bible, including Solomon's Temple (1 Kings 6:9-10), masts of ships (Ezekiel 27:5), wardrobes (Ezekiel 27:24), and even chariots (Song of Solomon 3:9).

Have you heard of a **cedar closet**? Cedar serves as an insulation from moisture, prevents mildew, keeps away moths, and has a wonderful, **sweet fragrance**. I think it's interesting that while King David was making plans to build the first temple for the Lord he said, "Here I am, living in a palace of **cedar**, while the ark of God remains in a tent" (2 Samuel 2:7). Although he was not allowed to build the temple, he gathered all the materials for his son Solomon to finish—and cedar was a **precious** addition.

Another fun fact is that cedar wood was used in Old Testament sacrifices. Animals were placed on cedar planks and burned. The fragrant smell of the cedar would fill the temple. Our fragrance also fills God's house as the sacrifice of our time, talents, and gifts are always a **pleasing aroma** to the Lord. Here is another metaphor of how **the tree** is used to bring glory to God. How cool!

• **The verse we are focusing on today is Psalm 92:12-15. Let's read it and once again see the PLANTED imagery.**

> • **Where are the palm and cedar trees PLANTED?**
>
> _____
>
> _____
>
> • **Where will they flourish?**
>
> _____
>
> _____
>
> • **What is significant about their old age?**
>
> _____
>
> _____
>
> • **What do they declare?**
>
> _____
>
> _____

Dr. Joe Temple makes a fascinating observation in his sermon titled *"Like a Palm Tree."* He points out the difference between where these trees are **planted** and where they **flourish.** The palm tree and the cedar are planted in the HOUSE of the Lord, but flourish in the COURTS of the Lord.

"If you are familiar with the Old Testament temple, you will know that the inner sanctuary was called the house of God, and the courts of the Lord was the outside. It was the yard so-to-speak. Nobody but the most high priest could come into the inner sanctuary— the house of God—but the ordinary folk, even the folk who were not Jews, even the folk who were not followers of God could come into the courts of the Lord on the outside… . A cedar tree and a palm tree has it's roots IN the house of God, but its branches and its fruit provide that which is needed by those who are on the OUTSIDE… . A Christian ought to be an individual whose roots are at the very heart of God, but (whose) branches are flourishing out into the courtyards where people are in need."[5]

Amazing, isn't it! Our tree is **PLANTED** in the very foundation and heart of the Lord. We are called to reach out to those in need and point them to the Lord, therefore; we should **reflect** and **imitate** who Jesus is. If He is called to bring freedom and good news for the oppressed, then we are to use our "branches" to reach out to those who need liberation in Christ! Read what Psalm 104:16-17 says about the cedar tree.

"The trees of the Lord are well watered, the **cedars** of Lebanon that he **planted.** There the birds make their nests …"

The bird in this passage is a sparrow. Can you recall the passage where Jesus tells us that not one sparrow will fall to the ground apart from the will of the Father? He goes on to tell us that all the hairs on our head are numbered, and we are not to be afraid because we are more important than the sparrow (Matthew 10:29-31). If we are well-watered cedar trees, sitting by the LIVING WATER and soaking up God's Word, we, too, will provide the shade for the sparrow and those who need **to rest** in the arms of Jesus. Today, let's make a commitment to STAND on Philippians 1:27.

"Just one thing: Live your life in a manner worthy of the gospel of Christ." (HCSB)

"The RIGHTEOUS FLOURISH like the PALM TREE and grow like a CEDAR in Lebanon. They are PLANTED in the house of the LORD; they FLOURISH in the courts of our God. They still bear FRUIT in old age; they are ever FULL of sap and green, to declare that the Lord is upright; he is my rock, and there is NO UNRIGHTEOUSNESS in him."

Psalm 92:12-15
(ESV)

Who are you providing shade for today? Believers in Christ, who are the righteousness of God, **GROW** like a cedar in Lebanon.

In closing, let's consider how cedars grow. They grow **SLOW.** There is no speedy cedar tree. Even the fruit of the cedar, known as a cedar cone, takes three years to grow into fruition. But when the fruit is ripe, the cone will burst into thousands of tiny seeds that are dropped to the ground where new cedar trees will grow.

Do you feel sometimes your growth in the Lord is taking TOO long? Are you frustrated when you cannot SEE the work of His hands?

> "Be STRONG and COURAGEOUS. Do not be terrified; do not be discouraged, for the LORD your God will be with you WHEREVER you go."
>
> Joshua 1:9

- **Let's look at the following verses and find courage and strength. Where does our strength lie?**

  - **Isaiah 30:15**
    Our strength lies in _____.

  - **Exodus 14:14**
    Our strength lies in _____.

  - **Joshua 1:9**
    Our strength lies in _____.

  - **1 Corinthians 16:13**
    Our strength lies in_____.

Our **strength** lies in the **confident trust** we have in the Lord! We can **STAND** on the Truth that God is at work, even when we can't see His hand. We can **REST** in the confidence that God is always fighting for us—we just need to STAND still, tall, and STRONG. Just like the cedar tree we, too, are emitting a sweet fragrance that is not only pleasing to God, but is also attracting others to Him. Isaiah 32:17 says:

> "The fruit of righteousness will be peace; the effect of righteousness will be quietness and confidence **forever**."

Just like the quiet, slow growth of the cedar, we can be confident that God is at work in us. Our shade can be a rest for others, and our fruit can be a fragrant offering of peace. When we are PLANTED in the house of God, we will make an impact for His Kingdom. And, at just the right time, God will use our gifts that will burst forth to spread the seeds of the gospel.

The main difference between the cedar and us? We won't live to see 2,000 years. We will live to see ETERNITY! Amen.

DAY FOUR/ THE PALM TREE

The palm tree is another beautiful picture of our Christian faith **STANDING** strong in the Lord. Palm trees in Scripture are thought to have had over 360 uses and can also be known as the "tree of life." We will never know if the palm was the true tree of life in the Garden of Eden, although we **do know** it meant **life** to many weary Israelites. The first mention of the palm is in Exodus 15:27. The Israelites had crossed over the Red Sea, traveled for days without water, and had finally come to Elim where they saw "twelve springs and seventy palm trees, and they camped there near the water." I would probably call it the tree of life too, after days of thirst and travel!

The fruit of the palm is called a **date,** the center is the **bud,** and the branches are known as **fronds** used for thatched roofs and baskets. The palm tree stands very **tall,** growing to heights of 80 to 90 feet. While both the oak and the cedar have a wide girth, the trunk of the palm tree does not change in thickness, but simply grows taller. If the main bud is damaged, the tree will die.

Like the limber pine, the palm tree is flexible in nature. It will not snap under harsh conditions and can handle the severity of storms because of its secure root system.

The palm tree is also a symbol of **victory** and was used as an ornamental design carved in many of the Temple decorations. One of the most famous display of palm branches was shown on what we now call Palm Sunday.

> • **Let's read about Christ's triumphal entry into Jerusalem from John 12:12-13.**
>
> > • **Why do you think the people met Jesus with palm fronds?**
>
> _____
>
> _____
>
> > • **What were they saying as He entered into Jerusalem?**
>
> _____
>
> _____

"The next day the great crowd that had come for the festival heard that Jesus was on his way to Jerusalem. They took PALM BRANCHES and went out to meet him, shouting, 'Hosanna!' 'Blessed is he who comes in the name of the Lord!' 'Blessed is the king of Israel!'"

John 12:12-23

At this time, Roman culture celebrated military victory with the laying down of palm branches. Some Israelites believed Jesus was the conquering King who had come to save them from Roman oppression. They believed Jesus came to victoriously set them free as a nation, rather than a spiritual King coming to save them from their sin. Therefore, this ancient tradition to lay palm fronds in front of a military leader signified the belief of some that day. However, Hosanna means "save us." Those who believed Jesus was the Messiah celebrated with palm fronds symbolizing the VICTORY of Old Testament prophecy fulfilled. Today, Palm Sunday ushers us into the Holy Week of Easter. We often wear the palm branch as a sign of the cross symbolizing Christ's victory over death and sin.

> • **Look up Revelation 7:9-12.**
>
> > • **Who do you see celebrating?**
>
> _____
>
> _____

Again we see the VICTORY of the Jesus, the Lamb of God, being celebrated with the use of palm branches. The difference is that a great multitude will be celebrating and honoring Him—one from every tribe and nation. There will be so many that no one can count.

• **Let's look at the verse we studied yesterday, Psalm 92:12-15.**

> "The righteous flourish like the palm tree and grow like a cedar in Lebanon.
> They are planted in the house of the Lord; they flourish in the courts of our God.
> They still bear fruit in old age; they are ever full of sap and green,
> to declare that the Lord is upright; he is my rock, and there is no unrighteousness in him."

Here we see the righteous flourishing like the palm tree.

• **What do you think the word "flourish" means?**

_____

_____

To flourish in Hebrew is *parach*. It means: to bud, to bloom, break out, to burst forth, to sprout.[6]

It also can mean: to grow or develop in a healthy or vigorous way, especially as the result of a particularly favorable environment.

• **From what you know about the palm tree combined with the definition of flourish, why do you think the Psalmist uses this illustration? Go back to your highlighted selections.**

_____

_____

_____

_____

_____

_____

I believe our Christian faith resembles the palm when we bloom where we are **PLANTED**. We flourish like the palm tree because we are growing **UP** in our faith. We have been **PLANTED** in favorable conditions, right by the edge of the streams of Living Water. We are fed everyday with the nourishment of the Word, and our roots are planted deep within the richness of the soil. We **flourish** because we, too, are limber like the elastic fibers of the palm. We take **delight** in the Lord by sitting at the river, and He gives us the desires of our hearts—our core, our bud. And when our bud is damaged, our whole tree is in jeopardy—just like the palm. This is why we wear our armor, our breastplate of righteousness, so we can protect the bud of our palm, our heart, against the forces of evil.

Most importantly, we wave our palm fronds and **stand** tall in the victory of Jesus.

•**What do the following verses teach about VICTORY in Christ?**

"But THANKS be to God, who GIVES us the VICTORY through our LORD JESUS CHRIST."

1 Corinthians 15:57

• **Psalm 40:1-4**

_____

_____

• **1 Corinthians 15:56-58**

_____

_____

• **2 Corinthians 2:14**

_____

_____

97

Victory in greek is *nikos*. Look familiar? It is where we get the word *Nike*. It means to utterly vanquish, overcome, death swallowed up in victory. When Jesus went to the cross to die for our sin, he **utterly vanquished** the wall that separated us from God forever. We **stand** TALL with PRAISE and THANKSGIVING, just like the palm tree, because Jesus is our Savior. Get out the palm branches. Here comes our King. The **victory is His.**

DAY FIVE/ THE OLIVE TREE

Today will be our last discussion on the symbolic trees found in Scripture and the characteristics they represent. I hope you have enjoyed this horticultural approach. Have you decided which tree was represented in Psalm 1:3 yet? Let's get started on day five.

The olive tree was considered by some to be the most valued tree in Palestine. It was called "the king of trees," and some traditions even believe THIS was the tree of life planted in the Garden of Eden. The olive tree was a symbol of beauty, strength, and peace. Its strong, beautifully-grained wood was used for the building of Solomon's Temple (1 Kings 6:23-35). The olive tree is also slow-growing and bears a bitter fruit known as the olive. The oil from olives had many uses. It was used for cooking, medicine (Luke 10:34), lighting, and the anointing of priests and kings (Exodus 29:7).

The first mention of this tree is in Genesis 8:11 when a dove returns to Noah carrying an olive branch in its mouth. It symbolizes peace on earth—the end of the flood and a new beginning for creation. The olive branch with thirteen leaves and thirteen olives is also found on the seal of United States of America.

While there is much to read about the olive tree and the production of olive oil, I would like us to focus on **two facts** I found very interesting in my study. I will call them **Lamp Lighting** and **Legacy Leaving.**

Lamp Lighting

In his article titled *the Mystery of the Olive Tree*, William Dankenbring tells us that the Hebrew word for olive tree is *es shemen,* which literally means **"tree of oil."** It is from the primitive root meaning **"to shine."** [6] The oil from the olive tree was the **source of light** providing fuel for lamps in ancient times. Olive oil is also symbolic of gladness and **joy.**

- **From these verses, what did olive oil represent?**

  - **Isaiah 61:3:** The oil of _____.
  - **Psalm 45:7:** The oil of _____.
  - **Psalm 104:14-17:** The oil makes his face _____.

- **What is JOY associated with in Galatians 5:22?**

  _____

- **Read Psalm 119:105. What lights our way?** _____

  "Your word is a lamp unto my feet and a light unto my path." Psalm 119:105

If we put all these Scriptures together, we come out with a beautiful, symbolic meaning for the olive tree. Stay with me here!

Olive tree means:"**TO SHINE.**"
    Oil is symbolic of **JOY.**
        Joy is a FRUIT of the **HOLY SPIRIT.**
            Oil is used in LAMPS.
                God's Word is the LAMP.

Dankenbring makes this conclusion from these truths:

"The oil of the lamp is the indwelling Spirit of God. God's Spirit sheds illumination on the laws and commandments of God giving us the understanding and wisdom and knowledge … . When a lamp is filled with oil, the wick maintains a steady flame until the fuel runs out. So it is with God's people. When we are filled with the Holy Spirit, our light shines **bright** and gives a steady radiant light!"

I think Dankenbring and I have the same idea. As we sit in God's presence and stand on His promises, we shine bright like the olive tree because we are being **fueled by the oil** of the Holy Spirit. We know from our **PLANTED** verse (Psalm 1:1-3) that when we delight in HIM, we are like a tree planted by streams of water that **yields our fruit** in season.

To yield means: to produce, to deliver.

God is **producing** the fruit of the Holy Spirit in us. Just as a lamp is filled with olive oil, we are being filled with God's Word and empowered by the fruit of the Spirit. Just as the lamp needs oil to maintain a steady glow, we, too, need to sit by the river daily to be fueled by the Word of God. And when we do, God's timing is always perfect. When I need a delivery of patience, He's right there. When I need a quick production of self-control, God's got it covered. Need some JOY today? Nehemiah 8:10 says, "The JOY of the Lord is your strength." Need some love? God will give you just what you need. How can this be? We produce fruit because we are attached to the Vine. Isn't this amazing? Who would have known we could glean so much from the olive tree?

Legacy Leaving

- **Please read Psalm 128:1-4.**

  - **What are described as olive plants here? Describe the mother.**

  _____

  _____

> "TEACH a youth about the way he should go; even when he is old he will not depart from it."
>
> Proverbs 22:6
> (HCSB)

This is the perfect place to insert the famous saying, *"The apple does not fall far from the tree"* … in a good sense! If you have children, you are called to raise them up in the Lord—to instruct them in the way they should go (Proverbs 22:6, Ephesians 6:4). I love the HCSB translation which emphasizes that we are to **TEACH** our children. You cannot teach what you do not know. Here we see that a mother who **remains connected** to the Vine, as we studied from John 15, **will be fruitful.** Not only that, her children will be fruitful and sprout up like olive shoots. Remember, the olive tree represents joy, gladness, light, and the fruit of the Holy Spirit. If the mom is sitting by the river and learning about Jesus, filling up with the Word, telling her children about the Lord, she is overflowing with goodness and leaving her family a **legacy of love.**

Isaiah 11:1 prophesies about Jesus as a shoot from the olive tree.

"… a shoot will come up from the stump of Jesse;
from his roots a Branch will bear fruit.
The Spirit of the Lord will rest on him—
the Spirit of wisdom and of understanding,
the Spirit of counsel and of might,
the Spirit of the knowledge
and fear of the Lord—and he will delight in the fear of the Lord."

Jesse was King David's father. Jesus, the Messiah, was foreseen to come from this family line. Read John 7:42.

> "Has not the Scripture said that the Christ comes from the offspring of David, and comes from Bethlehem, the village where David was?" John 7:42 (ESV)

One thing is clear. For Jesus to have been born from this family tree, we can be sure Jesse's mother did a good job of leaving her son and grandchildren a **LEGACY OF LOVE.** Yep, the apple doesn't fall far from the tree. Read Psalm 52:8 in the margin. Let's leave a legacy to our children by flourishing like the olive tree in the house of God.

In closing, there is plenty more to be studied about each of the five trees I have mentioned this week. But one **truth** ties them ALL together. Every tree mentioned was used to **build** the temple of the Lord.

Pine Tree: 1 Kings 9:10-11:

> "At the end of twenty years, during which Solomon built these two buildings--the temple of the LORD and the royal palace--King Solomon gave twenty towns in Galilee to Hiram king of Tyre, because Hiram had supplied him with all the **cedar and pine** and gold he wanted."

Palm Tree and Olive Tree: 1 Kings 6:31-35:

> "For the entrance to the inner sanctuary he made doors out of **olive wood** that were one fifth of the width of the sanctuary. And on the two olive-wood doors he carved cherubim, palm trees and open flowers, and overlaid the cherubim and **palm trees** with hammered gold."

Cedar Tree: 1 Kings 6:14-18:

> "So Solomon built the temple and completed it. He lined its interior walls with **cedar boards**, paneling them from the floor of the temple to the ceiling, and covered the floor of the temple with planks of juniper."

Do you see one missing? Yes, it's the oak of righteousness. Although this was not a wooden material used to build Solomon's temple, it is a spiritual quality needed for believers in Christ.

- **Please read 1 Corinthians 3:16.**
- **Who is the temple and where does God live?**

_____

_____

Solomon was building a house for the Lord, but today, we have even a better house for Him: **US**. God's spirit lives in each of us when we **believe** in His Son. We were once a wild olive shoot, but now we have been grafted onto the olive tree of Jesus.

We are His oaks of righteousness. We are His limber pine. We are His cedar of fragrant offering. We are His palm of victory. We are His olive tree of legacy. We are His trees.

Simply said … we are **PLANTED.**

Margin:

"But I am like an **olive tree** flourishing in the house of God; I trust in God's unfailing love for ever and ever. For what you have done I will always praise you in the presence of your faithful people. And I will hope in your name, for your name is good."

Psalm 52:8

"Don't you know that YOU YOURSELVES are GOD's TEMPLE and that God's Spirit LIVES IN YOU?"

1 Corinthians 3:16

VIEWER GUIDE: SESSION SEVEN
EVIDENCE OF HIS SPLENDOR

"They will be
called OAKS
of righteousness,
a PLANTING
of the Lord
for the display
of his
SPLENDOR."

Isaiah 61:3

Today we will look at FOUR ways we, as TREES, are a display of His splendor! Let's get started.

• We are the EVIDENCE of God's splendor.
Evidence means: the available information indicating whether a belief or position is _____.
We need to provide PROOF that we are a display of His splendor.

* FOUR ways we are PROOF of this LIVING TREE.

1. We are EVIDENCE of His splendor through our _____.

   • DELIGHT means: to mold, to bend, to be flexible.

Psalm 37:3-4
*"Trust in the Lord and do good; dwell in the land and enjoy safe pasture.
Take delight in the Lord, and he will give you the _____ of your heart."*

2. We are EVIDENCE of His splendor through our _____.

   • Our sufferings make us PAY ATTENTION to who He is.

   • Our sufferings remind us that God is more _____ than gold or silver.
      Ask yourself this question: **Is God Enough?**

   • Our sufferings remind us of who we are and what our mission is.

   • Our sufferings can also be EVIDENCE for someone else.

Psalm 119:74
*"May all who fear you find in me a cause for joy,
for I have put my hope in your word."*

   • Others will find joy when they see us because there is something different about us.

We will be different because our hope is not in our suffering, our hope is in the _____ .

3. We are EVIDENCE of His splendor through our life _____.

Proverbs 11:30
"The FRUIT of the righteous is a _____ of LIFE and the one who is WISE saves LIVES …"

• The trees of the Lord are WELL- _____, and the birds can rest in our trees!

• You can be PLANTED in the LIVING WATER or in the _____ _____.

4. We are EVIDENCE of His splendor through the light of our _____.

    • We are shining for the display of His splendor when we fill up with the Word of God.

    • The oil of the Holy Spirit lights our FAITH to be an evidence of His splendor.

• The **Limber Pine** teaches us to delight, to bend to God's ways.
• The **Oak of Righteousness** teaches us to stand firm; to be strong and courageous.
• The **Cedar** teaches us be a blessing for those around us.
• The **Palm** teaches us to walk in victory.
• The **Olive tree** teaches us that we are the OIL that SHINES.

We are the TREES of His splendor. We are living proof!

Isaiah 55: 11-13 (NLT)
"You will live in joy and peace. The mountains and hills will burst into song, and the trees of the field will clap their hands!
These events will bring great honor to the Lord's name; they will be an everlasting sign of his power and love."

NOTES:

WEEK EIGHT: Day One/ The Rescue

We made it to week eight! For the next three weeks, we will look at what it means to be **PLANTED** in our **WALK** with Jesus. The past seven lessons focused on SITTING and STANDING in our belief. Now we get to put "feet" to our faith and **WALK**.

Walking with Jesus is a beautiful picture of relationship, humility, love, practice, and discipline. God is in **deep pursuit** of us and desires we stay close and walk right beside Him. When our pace gets too fast, **He slows** us down. When we go ahead of Him and feel anxious, **He calls** us back. If we get lost, **He will** come and find us.

PLANTED is about sitting in God's presence FIRST. When we have rested and delighted in the truth of God's Word, then we are ready to STAND on His promises. The next step is **WALKING in His purposes.**

What are God's purposes anyway? How do I walk in them? What does walking in faith look like? We will answer these questions and more in the weeks to come.

Today, let's look at God's pursuit of us. It's called THE RESCUE.

> • **What does Psalm 37:23 say about God's pursuit? Read the NASB translation in the margin.**

_____

_____

"... He rescued ME, because He DELIGHTED in ME."

Psalm 37:23 (NASB)

God rescues us because He **delights** in us!

Did you get that? The Almighty, the Creator of Heaven and Earth delights in YOU and me. From what does He rescue us? First and foremost, He rescues us from our natural state of YUCK—that would be our sinful nature. Romans 5:8 tells us that "God **demonstrated** His own love for us in that while we were still sinners, Christ died for us." In other words, for no good reason, God loves us. Because He is absolutely CRAZY about us, He offers us His GRACE.

The word demonstrate means: to show, to place together, to STAND with.[1]

I love this definition because it fits right into our **PLANTED** study. God wants to STAND with us, so He proved His love by sending His Son. His love is beyond HUGE. It's ginormous.

> • **Read Ephesians 2:4-8. What did we DO to deserve God's love? From what are we being saved? (verse 5)**

_____

_____

_____

The mere fact that we get to SIT with God, STAND on His promises, and WALK in His purposes is **A GIFT**. We did NOTHING to earn it. Grace means showing unmerited favor. We, in and of ourselves, have done NOTHING or can do anything to earn God's grace or God's love. This is a hard concept for many people to understand because we live in a society that believes **performance = payment.**

"For it is by grace you have been saved, through **FAITH**—and this not from yourselves, it is the **gift** of God." Ephesians 2:8

Have you ever thought about these equations?

• How hard I work = How much money I will be paid.
• What I look like and how much personality I have = How well I am accepted.
• How my grades compare and how many extra curricular services hours I have = What college will accept me.
• What material possessions I have, the car I drive, the house I live in, my good health = How much God must favor me.

I've already confessed to you that I did not get in to college based on my stellar SAT scores. However, God did give me the gift of dance. At five-foot two, I entered Meadows School of the Arts at Southern Methodist University (SMU) on a classical Ballet scholarship. (My Dad was dancing, this time!) My freshman year, I read a book that changed my life—literally. It is called, *"The Search for Significance,"* by Robert McGee—*Seeing your true worth through the eyes of God.*

In his book, McGee makes a point that hit me to the core of my 18-year-old ballerina life. He says (paraphrasing), the Devil would like you to believe your entire self-worth is tied up in two things: **Appearance + the approval of others.** If you do not qualify under one of these two categories, you aren't of much value to anyone. On the other hand, McGee writes, GOD wants you to believe that you alone are created by HIS hand. **You are everything He has designed you to be**. You are His creation, and He loves you regardless of whether you have done this or that. You can do nothing to earn His love. It doesn't matter how smart you are, how much money you make, how funny you are, how well you dress, what car you drive, the house you live in, or that you can dance the *Bluebird Variation* from the ballet *Sleeping Beauty*! God loves you.

Some may say, "Well, that's great for you, Annie, but why would God **STAND** for me when I have made so many bad choices?

• **Read this encouragement in Romans 5:8 from** *The Message*:

> "But God put his love on the line for us by offering his Son in sacrificial death while we were of no use whatever to him." Romans 5:8

The reality is God does not need us. After all, He did a pretty good job with the creation of the world before we were born. The FACT is **He WANTS us** … warts and all! No matter what we have done, when we make the choice to believe in His Son, our once broken relationship with Him is now made **perfect.** We are His creation. We are His masterpiece. We are His children, and we are important to Him. He **demonstrates** His ultimate love for us through the life, death, and resurrection of Jesus (John 3:16). Yes, **He rescues us** from sin. But, He also rescues us from much more.

What about doubt? Worry? Fear? Depression? Financial stress? This idea of "rescue" is not of God swooping down to carry us away and solve all of our problems. He is not a magical genie that makes difficulty disappear. Instead, He promises to **WALK** with us through life and teach us along the way to TRUST in Him.

In a nutshell (yes, corny PLANTED imagery), GOD is in the job of **"rescue missions."** He pursues His children as He delights in us.

• **What does Zephaniah 3:17 say about this delight? What is your favorite part about this verse?**

_____

_____

_____

The NASB translation says:

> "The Lord God is in your midst. A VICTORIOUS warrior. He will exalt over you with joy. He will quiet over you with his love, He will rejoice over you with shouts of joy." Zephaniah 3:17

The idea of rejoicing reminds me of our son, Curry. He was six years old when we signed him up for his first year of basketball. His dad "Big Curry," was the coach. Needless to say, our son was not the most accurate ball shooter in this "pee wee" league. However, during one of the games, little Curry's shot miraculously found its way into the rim, and … he scored a basket. Without hesitation or thought, Curry made eye contact with his Dad, left the court mid-game, and ran to leap into his arms. (Of course, I am boo-hoo-ing on the side!)

What a day of rejoicing! What a day of victory! Our God is just like this! He will stop the game any day of the week for us to come, run, and jump into His arms. He takes **great delight** in us—when we make our first basket, when we get our first job, when we finish our project, even when we unload the dishwasher. His delight also extends to us when we don't feel pretty, worthy, or that we make any difference to anyone. God delights in us simply because we are **His.**

Did you know the international sign of surrender is to lift up your arms? In order to be rescued from our state of despair, we have to **lift up our arms and yield** to God's love and grace … just like the tree. We can do nothing to earn it.

It's a gift of His **grace.**
Are you ready to be rescued?

DAY TWO/ WALKING IN THE LIGHT

Let's begin today by opening our Bibles and sitting in the Word!

- **Looking up the following passages. What do they tell us about our WALK with the Lord?**

- **Psalm 16:11**

"The very
STEPS
we TAKE
come
from God;
otherwise how
would we
know where
we're going?"

_____

_____

_____

- **Proverbs 20:24**

_____

_____

_____

Proverbs 20:24
(MSG)

God knows the paths we are taking. He directs our way. He is our victorious warrior, and He is our perfect road map. When we follow His direction, our leaf does not wither, our fruit yields in season, and we prosper in all that we do (Psalm 1:3).

We studied Psalm 119:105 in week seven, but let's take another look.

"His word is a LAMP to my feet and a LIGHT for my PATH."

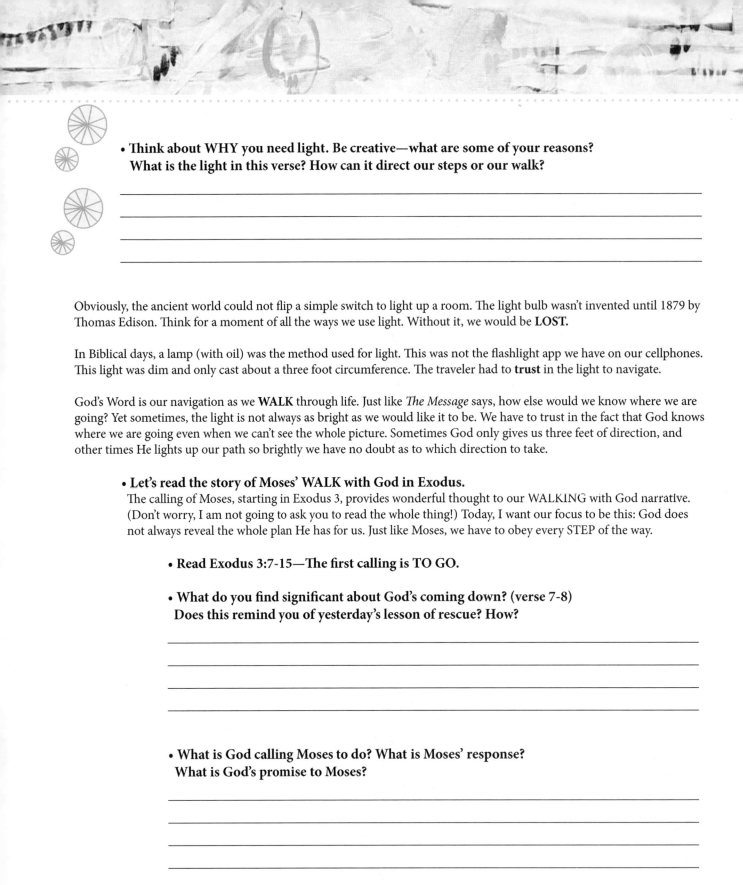

• **Think about WHY you need light. Be creative—what are some of your reasons?**
  What is the light in this verse? How can it direct our steps or our walk?

_____

_____

_____

_____

Obviously, the ancient world could not flip a simple switch to light up a room. The light bulb wasn't invented until 1879 by Thomas Edison. Think for a moment of all the ways we use light. Without it, we would be **LOST.**

In Biblical days, a lamp (with oil) was the method used for light. This was not the flashlight app we have on our cellphones. This light was dim and only cast about a three foot circumference. The traveler had to **trust** in the light to navigate.

God's Word is our navigation as we **WALK** through life. Just like _The Message_ says, how else would we know where we are going? Yet sometimes, the light is not always as bright as we would like it to be. We have to trust in the fact that God knows where we are going even when we can't see the whole picture. Sometimes God only gives us three feet of direction, and other times He lights up our path so brightly we have no doubt as to which direction to take.

• **Let's read the story of Moses' WALK with God in Exodus.**
  The calling of Moses, starting in Exodus 3, provides wonderful thought to our WALKING with God narrative. (Don't worry, I am not going to ask you to read the whole thing!) Today, I want our focus to be this: God does not always reveal the whole plan He has for us. Just like Moses, we have to obey every STEP of the way.

  • **Read Exodus 3:7-15—The first calling is TO GO.**

  • **What do you find significant about God's coming down? (verse 7-8)**
    Does this remind you of yesterday's lesson of rescue? How?

  _____

  _____

  _____

  _____

  • **What is God calling Moses to do? What is Moses' response?**
    What is God's promise to Moses?

  _____

  _____

  _____

  _____

Did God give Moses a public relation's strategy or a social media plan? Did God tell Moses how He was going to single-handedly save the Israelites from 500 years of slavery in Egypt? Did He provide Moses with information as to how **long** it would take? Do you see Moses punching the numbers, reviewing his assets, or weighing the costs? **NO. Moses simply obeyed and went.** God did not give Moses a business module. God's Word was enough to be the LIGHT unto Moses' path. God's Word was the way in which he would **WALK.** We should, too.

Do you ever find yourself doubting God's direction? Who am I Lord, that you would ask ME to do something like this? Have you ever felt like you were not good enough or qualified enough for the job? I can certainly identify with Moses. Here's a promise on which you can stand.

The I AM has sent you.
The I AM will be with you.
The I AM will teach you what to say and where to go.

Here are two Scriptures to memorize when you **think** you are alone.

"Now go; **I will help** you speak and will teach you what to say." Exodus 4:12

"… **I will help** … you speak and will teach you what to do." Exodus 4:15

Are you questioning the dimness of the light? Can you only see three feet in front of you? Don't fear. **I AM** came down from Heaven to rescue us, to HELP US, and to bring us out of the land of doubt and unbelief. He has come that we might have LIFE and have it abundantly (John 10:10). Matthew 1:23 says:

"The virgin will be with child and will give birth to a son, and they will call him Immanuel"
--which means, "God **with** us."

Notice the word WITH. Get ready to put on your sunglasses, because God's Word is about to SHINE. The greek word for **with** is *meta*. It signifies with, after, and behind. Let that sink in—SLOWLY.

WITH.
   AFTER.
      BEHIND.

Revelation 1:8 says:

"'I am the Alpha and Omega,' says the Lord God, 'who IS,
and who WAS, and who IS to come, the ALMIGHTY.'"

"I will walk AMONG YOU and be YOUR God, and YOU will be MY people."

Leviticus 26:12

The I AM is WITH you. He is with you to WALK **with** you. He is with you to walk **after** you. He is with you to walk **behind** you. He NEVER leaves your side. NEVER. God is with you even when you cannot see the road ahead.

God is with you.

Do you have tough decisions to make this week? God is with you even when you don't feel like you fit the job description.

• **Let's close by reading Leviticus 26:12. Reflect on these words and write a prayer of surrender.**

_____

_____

_____

Walk worthy of the KING today. The Lord taught Moses step-by-step, and He will do the same with you. Put on your sunglasses. Let's WALK in the LIGHT of His Word.

Day Three/ He SEES me in the DARKNESS

Today, we are going to look at the story of Hagar. Hagar was an Egyptian maidservant that belonged to Sarah (at this time, called Sarai), Abraham's wife. We find in Genesis 16 that Sarah did not have any children (even though God had promised Abraham descendants in Genesis 12). Because Sarah was barren and impatient, she gave Hagar to Abraham to be his wife. (Note: although this sounds horrific in our culture today, this was not an uncommon practice in the ancient world.) Abraham consented, and Hagar conceived a child—which made Sarah furious. Her jealousy rose to such a level that she began to despise Hagar. Sarah mistreated her to the point that Hagar fled into the desert. In Genesis 16, we find Hagar alone and ready to die. We also find God in **deep pursuit** of His lost child.

- **Read Genesis 16:7-15.**

    - **Who appeared to Hagar? What did He say to her?**

    _____

    _____

    _____

    _____

    - **How does this prove that God knows the steps of our lives—our walk?**

    _____

    _____

    _____

    _____

God told Hagar to return to her mistress. Why in the world would God tell her to return to an abusive situation? God **had a plan.** He had a plan for Sarah, and He had a plan for Hagar. We will have a better understanding of Hagar's journey back home when we look more closely at the word **return.**

This word in Hebrew is: *shuwb* meaning to restore, to allow to return.[2]

The idea behind this concept is this: Hagar was NOT returning alone. She was returning **WITH** God. God would be in her midst. God would indwell her inner being and be with her thoughts and emotions. God was behind her and would go before her. He reminded Hagar that HE would be the one to increase her descendants, and they would be too many to count. In her obedience, Hagar returns to Sarah and gives the name to the Lord, "You are the God who sees me," for she said, 'I have now seen the One who sees me" (Genesis 16:13).

Where was Hagar when the Angel of the Lord found her? She was by a spring in the desert. Hagar was a lonely tree planted by streams of water. The spring of water nourished her soul as the LIVING God refreshed her broken heart.

THE SPRING OF WATER NOURISHED HER SOUL

- **From the following verses, what hope do you find?**

    - **Isaiah 41:18**

    _____

    _____

- **Isaiah 43:19**

_____

_____

"SEE,
I AM
doing a NEW
thing! Now it
SPRINGS up;
do you not
perceive it?
I AM
making a way in
the desert
and STREAMS
in the
wasteland."

Isaiah 43:19
(HCSB)

See, **I AM** doing a new thing!

God was taking Hagar's desert and turning it into streams of **living** water. He took her brokenness and dire situation and changed it for a **hopeful** future. God pursues the heavily-burdened, the weak, and the weary. God also pursues the joyful and the obedient. He sees us, hears us, and has compassion on us. He knows our steps, directs our ways, and **stands** with us. His deep pursuit covers all our needs. When we have no idea where we are going, He will take us by the hand and WALK WITH us.

Trusting God is never more real than when you need His direction.

- **What are you experiencing today that requires God to go WITH you?**

_____

_____

_____

_____

Maybe you are making a decision about a job change. Perhaps you are asking God to give you wisdom about a relationship. Are you looking for direction about raising your children? Are you trying to care for an ailing parent? Do you need marital advice? Are you experiencing financial stress?

God is **alive** IN YOU. His Spirit is **working** IN YOU. If you are **sitting** with Him each morning and **standing** on the promises of His Word, then LISTEN to the nudges of your heart. They could be lighting a direction for you.

God promises in Isaiah 30:21:

"Your own ears will hear him. Right behind you a voice will say,
'This is the way you should go,'
whether to the right or to the left." (NLT)

This is another promise on which we can **stand**. We probably will not hear an audible voice, but in our spirits, we will know the direction in which God wants us to go. If this concept seems vague to you, remember the verses we studied as we SAT with the Lord.

- Do not worry. (Philippians 4:6)
- Come to Me all who are weary and I will give you rest. (Matthew 11:28)
- Trust in Me. (John 7:38)
- I am fighting for you. (Exodus 14:14)
- I will direct you and teach you the way you should go. (Psalm 32:8)
- Ask for wisdom, and I will give it to you generously without finding fault. (James 1:5)
- Cast your cares upon Me. (1 Peter 5:7)
- Delight yourself in Me, and I will give you the desires of your heart. (Psalm 37:4)

Remember these words are life, and they are LIGHT as we WALK with the Lord. They protect us from unseen obstacles. They light up danger ahead. They give us discernment. They offer us peace. They illuminate our decisions. They search our hearts. They expose our motives. They brighten our confidence. They give us power to STAND on His promises so we can **WALK** in His purposes.

What is going on in your life today?
The I AM sees you and knows EXACTLY what you need. Trust Him with your next steps.

Close today by praying Psalm 23. This Psalm fits perfectly in our study of walking with our Shepherd. He knows our voice. He sees us. He rescues us. He **deeply pursues** us.

Lord, thank You that You are my Shepherd. Help me not to be distracted by the things in this world that grab my attention.
I know that You are watching over me and taking care of my every need. Why would I ever want more?
I pray You will lead me to those places of quiet when life gets too busy. I pray You will restore me when life gets too full.
I pray You will guide me to the paths of righteousness when I might want to go another way.
You are WITH me Lord, always. Even when I WALK through difficult situations, You are WITH me.
I will not be afraid, because You are WALKING right by my side. You know my name, and You know my steps.
Lead me, teach me, and guide me in the way I should go. Amen.

DAY FOUR/ MARVELOUSLY HELPED

For the past three days we have studied God's **deep pursuit** of us. The Lord of Heaven and Earth desires we walk close with Him—not because He needs us, but because He wants us. He gives us the Holy Spirit so we can sense His holy nudges and **WALK** in the light of His direction.

> • **Read the following verses. What does God say is absolutely essential about our character when we walk with Him?**
>
> > • **Psalm 25:9**
> >
> > _____
> > _____
> >
> > • **Isaiah 66:2**
> >
> > _____
> > _____

Humility is required when we walk with God. Humility is meekness, not weakness. When we are humble before the Lord, we realize there is nothing we have done or nothing we can do to earn God's love. As we learned in day one, God's love is a gift of GRACE. Humility is being **poor** before the Lord.

> • **What were Jesus' words to His disciples as He began His ministry in Matthew 5:3?** (This is the beginning of His teaching known as the Sermon on the Mount.)
>
> _____
> _____

The Beatitudes are foundational to Jesus' teachings. They are **"beautiful attitudes"** the Christian is to exemplify as we WALK with Him. *Blessed* simply means the ability to experience ultimate JOY in the Lord regardless of our circumstances. It is the same word used in Psalm 1:1—*"Blessed* are those …*."* In Matthew 5:3, the believers in Christ are blessed because they are poor in spirit. Poor means: "empty, destitute, nowhere to turn."[3] In other words, we are blessed when we **empty** ourselves before our mighty God. When we do this, God fills us up with His guidance and teaches us the way we should go.

"He GUIDES
the HUMBLE
in what is RIGHT
and TEACHES
them HIS
way."

Psalm 25:9
(NLT)

My Bible study teacher and good friend, Neely Towe, used an excellent image to explain being "poor" in spirit. She equated being poor to filling up her car with gasoline. Let me explain. Neely was using a lower octane gas only to find her car beginning to "knock." Her husband explained that her car did not need mechanical work, but that the gas and air mixture was just not burning as **intended**. Being low in fuel, she decided to mix higher premium gas with the lower octane. The trusty 'ole car still knocked. Her conclusion? She would have to empty her tank COMPLETELY before she could fill it up with the higher octane fuel.

We are the same way. Remember, being poor in spirit is emptying ourselves and allowing God's Word to fill us—clearly with high octane gasoline. But our culture likes to mix a little of this with a little of that. We like to mix a little of the world's philosophy with the parts of the Bible we "like." We like to mix a little of our agenda with God's plans. We like to share the glory and take more credit than we ought. Or, we take a shortcut all together and make plans without Him. But guess what happens? We start **to knock.** We are not living as intended. We begin to make noises that are NOT of God, and our fragrance begins to sputter smoke and fumes. In time, the efficiency of our engine, our heart, starts to feel the damage. We are no longer poor in spirit but full of ourselves. This is not how God intended us to walk … or drive.

King Uzziah is a great example of what happens when you shift from high octane to lower than low.

- **Read the story of King Uzziah's walk with the Lord in 2 Chronicles 26:3-21.**

    - **What happened when the King sought the Lord? (verse 5)**

    _____

    - **What happened when the King got too full of himself? (verses 16-21)**

    _____

    _____

    - **2 Chronicles 26:15 says, "He was greatly helped until he became powerful."
    Who helped him become powerful? When did the shift from humility to pride happen?**

    _____

    _____

    _____

The opposite of humility is arrogance and **pride.** We cannot be humble and full of ourselves at the same time. Just like lower and higher octane gas, the two do not mix. While the King was **WALKING** with the Lord, God gave him **success.** The King James Version says, "God made him **to prosper.**" I hope this rings a bell to remind you of our foundational verse.

"He is like a tree planted by streams of water, which yields its fruit in season and whose leaf does not wither. **Whatever he does prospers.**" Psalm 1:3

When God is with us, whatever we do will prosper. If we are delighting in Him, He will give us the desires of our heart. The question is: Where are we on the humble scale?

- **Ranging from one to ten, how humble are you about your successes in life? Circle one.**

    1   2   3   4   5   6   7   8   9   10

- **What is the adjective used in verse 15 that describes how King Uzziah was helped?**

_____

Some versions of the Bible say that the King was greatly helped or strongly helped. Most versions say that Uzziah was **MARVELOUSLY helped.**

Marvelously is *pala*, meaning:

> to be marvelous, be wonderful, be extraordinary, to do an extraordinary or a hard or a difficult thing, **beyond one's power to do.**[4]

What extraordinary things did God do in King Uzziah's life? Look at his record! He won wars with his well-trained army, rebuilt towns, built towers, dug cisterns, provided spears, helmets, coats of armor, bows, built catapults, and more!

Who gave him this extraordinary reputation and blessed him with success? Who gave him success beyond what he had the power to do himself? It's a three letter word. **G-O-D.**

- **Think back on your week. How has God marvelously helped you?**

_____

_____

_____

> "And his name spread far abroad; for he was **MARVELOUSLY HELPED,** till he was STRONG."
>
> 2 Chronicles 26:15

God marvelously helped him as long as he **sought** the Lord. This is the point where we will plant ourselves for the rest of our lesson. Remember (week two, day five, pg. 25), that to seek (sought) is *darash* meaning:

> to seek, to inquire, to search, to investigate, to seek with care, to frequent a place, to ask, to practice, to study, to follow, to rub.[4]

- **Whew! That's a long list of words. Which one resonated with you?**
  As long as King Uzziah _____ the Lord, He gave him success.

I like the phrase "to rub." It makes me think of Silly Putty.™ As a child, I used the putty to make "prints" of things. Newspaper always worked the best! Simply rubbing the putty on newspaper would give you an exact print. Using this imagery, when we **sit** at the Lord's feet, **stand** on His promises, and **WALK** in His purposes, He rubs off on us. We are His print. We are His image.

I will close today with an excerpt from *Streams in the Desert* from September 18th.

> *"The amount of time we spend before God is critical, for our hearts are like photographer's film— the longer exposed, the deeper the impression. For God's vision to be impressed on our hearts, we must sit in stillness at His feet for quite a long time. Remember, the troubled surface of a lake will not reflect an image."* [6]

I guess the opposite works just as well, too. The longer we are exposed to the world's thinking, the more we are impressed with a "do it your way" attitude. Be careful. Proud thinking can lead us to be a leprous tree in no time. This is not the walk God intended for you. Don't mix the world's messages into the truth of Scripture. Make right decisions and lasting impressions. Don't let your heart start knocking. The only knocking God wants to hear is your heart knocking at His door. He's there and waiting. Let's walk on in.

> "Here I am! I stand at the door and knock. If anyone hears my voice and opens the door, I will come in and eat with him, and he with me." Revelation 3:20

DAY FIVE/ HE WALKS WITH ME

For our last day of study, we will take a closer look at the word **PROSPER**—in times of success and in times of sorrow. Our character study will focus on the life of Joseph. His **WALK** and beautiful attitude in Genesis is the perfect illustration to show us that when we stay close to God, whatever we do **will** prosper. We saw yesterday, from King Uzziah's example, that when we turn our focus away from God and onto ourselves, we no longer have the marvelous help.

> **• What are our instructions in the following verses in order that we may prosper?**

> **• Joshua 1:8**
>
> _____
>
> _____

"Do not let this Book of the Law depart from your mouth; MEDITATE on it day and night, so that you may be CAREFUL to do everything written in it. Then you will be PROSPEROUS and SUCCESSFUL."

Joshua 1:8

> **• Deuteronomy 29:9**
>
> _____
>
> _____

The word **prosper** in Hebrew is *tsalach*, a verb meaning:

> to advance, to make progress, succeed, to be profitable.

• What does Jeremiah 29:11 say about the word prosper?

_____

_____

> "'For I know the plans I have for you,' declares the LORD,
> 'plans to prosper you and not to harm you, plans to give you hope and a future.'"

Our job is to be a tree PLANTED. We must dig our roots deep and not let God's Word depart from our mouths. We must carefully follow the words in Scripture so we will not miss out on the many blessings God has for us. He knows the plans He has for us, plans to **prosper** us and not to harm us—all the days of our lives. I don't know about you, but I find PEACE and REST in this concept.

• What do the following verses say about God's faithfulness?

• 1 Corinthians 10:13

_____

_____

• Matthew 6:13

_____

_____

• 2 Thessalonians 3:3

_____

_____

Understanding God's faithfulness is a perfect background as we begin to study the life of Joseph. Joseph's life illustrates the picture of **WALKING** with God and being prosperous, even when trouble is evident. Joseph sought the Lord and was marvelously helped. He kept his eyes on God and trusted in His Hand as he **walked.**

Let's quickly review. Joseph was born to Jacob and Rachel and had 10 older brothers and one little brother, Benjamin. Joseph had a slightly pious character growing up and because Jacob favored Joseph, his older brothers despised him. Hmmm—sound familiar? Instead of Joseph fleeing into the desert like Hagar, Joseph's brothers sold him to slave traders headed to Egypt. The brothers faked his death and told their father he had been killed by a wild animal.

Our story picks up just as Joseph has been sold to Potiphar.

> • **Open your Bible and read Genesis 39:1-5.**
> • **How does this story connect us to Psalm 1:1-3?**

_____

_____

_____

_____

_____

_____

_____

"No temptation has seized you except what is common to man. And God is FAITHFUL; he will NOT let you be tempted BEYOND what you can bear. But when you are tempted, he will also PROVIDE a way out so that you can STAND UP under it."

1 Corinthians 10:13

"**The Lord was with** Joseph so that he **prospered**, and he lived in the house of his Egyptian master. When his master saw that the Lord was with him and that the Lord gave him success in everything he did, Joseph found favor in his eyes and became his attendant. Potiphar put him in charge of his household, and he entrusted to his care everything he owned." Genesis 39:2-4

"Blessed is the one who does not **walk** in step with the wicked or **stand** in the way that sinners take or **sit** in the company of mockers, but whose delight is in the law of the Lord, and who meditates on his law day and night.
That person is like a tree **planted** by streams of water,
which yields its fruit in season
and whose leaf does not wither—
whatever they do prospers." Psalm 1:1-3

In the next scene, we find Joseph betrayed by Potiphar's wife and thrown into jail because he would not disrespect Potiphar and sleep with her.

> • **Read Genesis 39:20-23. How can you make the connection here with our PLANTED verse?**

_____

_____

_____

Joseph's life is a **living example** of how we will prosper when God's hand is upon us—in good times and in hard times. God's marvelous help allows us to prosper **even in** tough situations. Joseph was sold into slavery, then taken to the top management position of Potiphar's house. He was sent to prison for two years, then placed second in command after interpreting a dream for Pharaoh. Because Joseph trusted in God, God **marvelously helped** him, prospered him, and sustained him **step-by-step.**

Joseph's rollercoaster life was all part of God's plan. God foreknew the Israelites would need to move to Egypt because of a famine, and Joseph would be in charge to take care of his family when they arrived. We also know Joseph trusted in God's plan because of his response to his brothers when they discovered he was ALIVE!

"'So Joseph said to his brothers, 'Come near to me, please.' And they came near. And he said, 'I am your brother, Joseph, whom you sold into Egypt. And now do not be distressed or angry with yourselves because you sold me here, for God sent me before you to preserve life. For the famine has been in the land these two years, and there are yet five years in which there will be neither plowing nor harvest. And God sent me before you to preserve for you a remnant on earth, and to keep alive for you many survivors.'"
Genesis 45:4-7 (ESV)

"You intended to harm me, but God intended it for GOOD to accomplish what is now being done, the saving of many lives." Genesis 50:20

> • **How about you? Do you trust God when you are going through a tough time? Do you believe His hand is on YOU as you WALK with Him? Is there a purpose for your suffering as there was for Joseph?**

_____

_____

_____

I heard a song the other day by Natalie Grant, called *Desert Song*. The song is about **praying** when life seems dry and **trusting** when life seems to have lost its hope. It is a reminder that God is the One who provides. God is the One who WALKS with us when life gets messy. God is our victory, and He will never leave us. The very last words stopped me in my tracks:

"I know I'm filled to be emptied again. The seed I've received, I will sow." [8]

Every day we must come before the Lord and **empty** ourselves. We need to sit by the stream and be ready to be **filled.** God has given us all a seed to sow. He has given us talents, gifts, and resources that are to be used for His glory. He has PLANTED us with a PURPOSE, and we were made to PROSPER.

Let's close this week by meditating and delighting on perhaps another familiar song, *In the Garden.* As we sing silently together, let's focus on the third stanza.

And He walks with me, and He talks with me,
And He tells me I am His own;
And the joy we share as we tarry there,
None other has ever known.

I'd stay in the garden with Him
Though the night around me be falling,
But He bids me go; through the voice of woe
His voice to me is calling. [9] *C. Austin Miles*

He is calling us to WALK in the garden each morning. He wants us to **sit** in His presence, **stand** on His promises, and **WALK** in His purposes. Do you hear the sweet sound of His voice? Let's walk today TRUSTING we are in the palm of His hands. Thank you, Lord. Amen.

VIEWER GUIDE: SESSION EIGHT
WALKING IN THE POWER OF NOW

This is our first week of WALKING into the purposes of God.

The Bible is filled with REAL stories of REAL people in their REAL walk with God.
These characters SAT in God's presence, STOOD on His promises, and WALKED in His purposes.

1. When we are CALLED to something, God will equip us with His _____ to accomplish it.

> "So then, just as you received Christ Jesus as Lord, continue to live your lives in him, rooted and built up in him, strengthened in the faith as you were taught, and overflowing with thankfulness. "
>
> Colossians 2:6-7

Philippians 1:6
"Being confident of this, that He who began a good work in you, will carry it on to completion until the day of Christ Jesus."

2. God INVITES us to be used by Him. Why does He invite us? Because He _____ in us.

3. We have been saved by _____ alone. There is NOTHING we have done to deserve the incredible gift of Jesus. He is WITH us. He takes great DELIGHT in us. And He rejoices over us with _____.

4. God is WALKING WITH us. Meta means: with, after, and _____. We find God in the present moment. Today is the perfect present.

- **GOD WANTS TO WALK WITH US IN THE PRESENT MOMENT.**

5. God simply told Moses to _____, and I will be WITH you. God is in the present moment of the I AM.

- **GOD HAS A MUCH BIGGER PLAN.**

6. We must KEEP WALKING when life gets hard and people disagree with us.

7. God made it very clear to Moses that He was the I AM. Moses made it clear to the Israelites that God was the I AM. Through the plagues, God made it clear to the Egyptians that HE WAS THE I AM. Through Moses' obedience, our generation knows that GOD is the I AM!

8. One person WALKING in obedience can make THE difference! It all begins with our _____.

9. He has chosen ALL of us to _____ before Him, to _____ Him, and to minister before Him. We have the power to make the difference in someone's life, too!

10. We are delighting in God as HE is delighting in us. Let us stand FIRM and WALK.

2 Chronicles 29:11
"My sons, do not be negligent now, for the Lord has chosen you to stand before him and serve him, to minister before him and to burn incense."

NOTES:

Last week we looked at the different ways people **WALKED** with God. This week we will focus on **HOW** we **WALK** with God using Jesus as our fearless leader. The ways we are instructed to WALK with God are no different than what He asked of His own Son, Jesus.

Walk in **humility**. Jesus walked as a humble servant.
Walk with a **thankful** and **trusting** heart. Jesus never once doubted the direction of God.
Walk in **obedience**. Check. He did that too.
Walk in the face of **suffering**? Got it.
Walk when you are **uncertain** of the future?
Walk even when you don't want to?

Jesus walked every path you and I will ever venture to tread. Let's look to Him to be our guide this week ... and in every week to come.

> • **What does Micah 6:8 say about walking with God?**

_____

_____

> • **Why do you think humility is important in our walk with God?** (Hint: look back over your notes from last week ... King Uzziah)

_____

_____

The idea that GOD wants to walk with US is beyond my comprehension this morning! In this passage, Micah is telling us that God is MOST pleased when we come to Him with a humble spirit over ANY other sacrifice.

Psalm 51:17 says:

> "The sacrifice pleasing to God is a broken spirit.
> God, You will not despise a broken and humbled heart." (HCSB)

A broken and contrite heart portrays the idea of someone who is **humble** in heart. Humility is simply to be lowly, to depress, to be modest.

I love the idea of de-**press**. When you de-press something, you make it smaller; you reduce it. This concept of "de-pression" is not about God wanting to lower our spirits or make our days sad and gloomy. On the contrary, God wants us to be humble so He can fill us up to the fullness of Him (Ephesians 3:19). Remember last week's analogy of the gas tank? If we have pride or arrogance in our lives, He has no place to fill because we are "full of ourselves." God wants us to **press into Him** so He can make an im-pression upon our souls and expose us to His ways (like the photographer's film). This means we have to de-press or **humble** ourselves.

> • **What does Philippians 3:12-14 say about pressing?**

_____

_____

- **How do we do this? Why are we doing this?**

_____

_____

We are pressing to take HOLD of what Christ has already taken hold of for us. He has saved us from our sin, given us new life, and promised us eternal life with Him. I would say that is some kind of prize to win!

- **How are you pressing to WIN the prize today?**

_____

_____

Think about the word **win** for a moment. For all of you competitive women out there, you will stop at nothing to WIN the prize … **any** prize (even if you are winning "Bananagrams" against your 10-year-old). The NIV study notes says, "This Christian life is like a race, and Paul's goal is Christ's goal for him, and Christ supplies the resources for him to 'press on toward the goal.'" [1]

- **What do you think is Christ's goal for you? How is He supplying the resources?**

_____

_____

- **Can you honestly say your goal is Christ's goal or do you have a secret agenda?**

_____

_____

Christ's goal for each of us is different because we are ALL created with different gifts and talents. However, we do have a common goal to WIN. We need to live this life with HUMILITY, with thanksgiving, with trust, with love, and with forgiveness.

- **Fill in the blanks. We need to live this life with** _____.

Do you know the best part? Christ is giving us the resources **to sit, to stand, and to walk** in order to win this race!

- **Read 2 Peter 1:3** in the margin.

God gives us ALL the resources we need. But what is the ONE thing that can keep us stuck in the mud from winning the race? It is called our **past.**

A major component to winning the race is **forgetting what is behind**—forgetting our **past** and letting go so Christ can fill us up. Why is this so difficult?

One thing is for certain, our past can be a happy memory or it can be a anchor in our soul from which we cannot be released. Paul is not telling us to completely forget our past. Instead, Paul is telling us that in order to move forward toward the goal, we must leave the past by the river where Jesus can wash us clean.

Do you remember week four when we talked about the word **overlook**? I'll refresh your memory. Overlook means:

> to pass over, to forgive, to CROSS OVER AS OF A RIVER, to go away.

"By his DIVINE POWER, God has given us EVERYTHING we need for LIVING a GODLY life. We have received all of this by COMING to know him, the one who CALLED us to himself by means of his marvelous GLORY and EXCELLENCE."

2 Peter 1:3 (NLT)

We discussed earlier the need to cast our concerns upon the foot of the cross where we are completely forgiven, **forever.** We talked about waking up each morning and doing our "laundry" in the river and letting God wash us clean. This might spark your memory. **Rise ye up**—take your journey and cross over the river!

Rise ye up! Don't let the past weigh you down from winning the race to which GOD Himself has called you. Winning takes **humility**. It takes knowing and believing God is the One who gives us the knowledge, the strength, the patience, the desire, the courage, and the passion. I believe remembering your past keeps you humble. I also believe Christ can use your past to minister to others. Being humble is knowing and believing that Christ took your past and made you into a NEW creation.

"Therefore, if ANYONE is IN Christ, he is a NEW creation; the old has GONE, the NEW has COME!"

2 Corinthians 5:17

• **Let's close today by looking at two verses.**

• **Read 2 Corinthians 5:17. What is the promise?**

_____

_____

• **Read Isaiah 43:18-19. What is the instruction?**

_____

_____

My husband had to get a new car last year because his old car was flooded in one of Florida's tropical storms. While driving one day, I noticed I was looking for his old car and not his new one. It was just routine. It was familiar. Every time I would see the make of his old car, I would look for him. Of course he was not in it. HE GOT A NEW CAR. The thought occurred to me that even though we are made NEW in Christ, we tend to look for our old past behaviors. They are routine, and they are familiar. However, **we are made NEW in Jesus.** Sit on that for a minute. We no longer have to dwell on our past mistakes, our past choices, and our past decisions. Why? We are being made **NEW**.

Ezekiel 36:26 says:

"I will give you a new heart and put a new spirit in you; I will remove from you your heart of stone and give you a heart of flesh."

Stop looking for your old car! I promise the new one will never be flooded out! You need to make sure you use the right gas and check it often, too. What grade is it? Make sure you are running on **HUMILITY.**

DAY TWO/ WALKING IN HIS LIKENESS

Yesterday, we learned to leave our past behind and only run on **humility**. Today, we will continue to explore WALKING in humility by looking at Christ as an example. I want to start again with the word **humble**.

The term "humility" comes from the latin word "humilitas" meaning "grounded," "from the earth," or "low," since it derives from humus meaning earth. [2] Human also comes from the latin word humus. Out of this we get the word homo, meaning man.

• **Do you see the connection between HUMble, HUMus, and HUMan? What is your conclusion?**

_____

_____

_____

We all know these three words start with HUM. More importantly, they all have something to do with being **low to the ground**. I am sure you have heard the saying, "dumb as dirt." In humility, we need to be "low as dirt!"

- **Let's take a quick look back in Genesis to the Garden of Eden. Read Genesis 2:7, 3:8-12.**

  - **Where did we come from in Genesis 2:7?**

    _____

    _____

  - **What was God doing in Genesis 3:8?**

    _____

    _____

  - **What was man doing in Genesis 3:10?**

    _____

    _____

  - **Why was man fearful of God?**

    _____

    _____

These verses beautifully tie together our concept of walking in humility before God. Why? We need a **holy fear** of the Lord in order to walk humbly before Him.

- **Look at Deuteronomy 10:12-13.**

- **What is God asking of us in order to walk humbly with Him?**

  _____

  _____

If we do not have a healthy FEAR of the Lord and walk in holy respect, we will never walk believing that He is supreme. This type of fear is not an "I'm scared out of my pants" fear, but rather a holy reverence, to be held in awe, to be awed, to have honor for. This fear of the Lord makes us bend low and walk with humility before Him. In comparison with His majesty, we have no chance of measuring up.

- **Let's take a look at Jesus in Philippians 2:5-11.**

- **How is He our example of how to walk with humility and reverence?**

  _____

  _____

  _____

  _____

  _____

"Now, Israel, what does the Lord your God require from you, but to FEAR the Lord your God, to WALK in ALL His ways and LOVE Him, and to SERVE the Lord your God with ALL your heart and with ALL your soul, and to KEEP the Lord's commandments and His statutes which I am commanding you today for your good?"

Deuteronomy 10:12-13 (NASB)

121

I love what *The Message* says:

> "He didn't claim special privileges. Instead, he lived a selfless, obedient life
> and then died a selfless, obedient death—." Philippians 2:8

When you are humble, you don't claim any special privileges. You live placing other's needs before your own.

- **What do these verses say about putting others interests above yours?**

> "Do NOTHING
> out of SELFISH
> ambition
> or VAIN conceit.
> Rather, in
> **HUMILITY**
> value others
> ABOVE yourselves,
> not looking to your
> OWN interests
> but each of you to
> the interests of the
> OTHERS."
>
> Philippians 2:3-4

- **Philippians 2:3-4**

_____

_____

- **Romans 12:10**

_____

_____

- **John 13:34-35**

_____

_____

JESUS' ONLY AGENDA WAS GOD'S AGENDA

It is only with **humility** and a **holy fear** of the Lord that we can consider other's needs over our own. I think there is a reason that human, humus, and humility all derive from the same root. We come from the ground and need to stick low to it. As soon as we think we are high and mighty, we fill ourselves with pride and arrogance. Who wants to be around a tree like that?

I want to be a tree that keeps her limbs low to the ground. I want to be rooted in the earth, filling my soul with the refreshing water of the Spirit, and displaying all of God's splendor. Jesus was like this, so let's take our lead from Him. He wasn't proud but always sought to humble Himself for others. He feared the Lord, walked in all of His ways, loved Him, and served Him with ALL of His heart, soul, mind, and strength. Jesus' only agenda was God's agenda. Because of this holy reverence and obedience, we, too, can **walk in His likeness** … and bow down, low.

DAY THREE/ WALKING IN THANKSGIVING

Today, we are going to keep it short and sweet! (Maybe more sweet than short.) We are told **many** times in the Bible to WALK with thankful hearts, always giving God the praise and glory. Today, we will discover why.

- **The first verse I want us to study is Hebrews 13:15-16.**

  - **What are we to continually offer God?**

  _____

  _____

• **What are we also NOT to forget?**

_____

_____

We find in these verses that God is pleased when we offer **a sacrifice of praise.** Why would bringing God our glory be considered a sacrifice? **First**, the offering of gratitude and keeping a humble heart is considered a sacrifice that is pleasing to God. We confirmed this on day one (Psalm 51:17). **Second,** an attitude of thankfulness and praise is a form of **obedience.** We can follow God's rules all day long, but without a thankful heart, we are missing the point. Notice Hebrews 13:15-16 says, "Through JESUS" we are offering UP a sacrifice of praise ... giving THANKS ... not neglecting doing good ... and sharing with others. Thankfulness and obeying God go hand in hand. It's the proof of our faith in action (James 2:22-24).

The Message says:

"Make sure you don't take things for granted and go slack in working for the common good; share what you have with others. God takes particular pleasure in acts of worship— a different kind of "sacrifice"—that take place in kitchens and workplace and on the streets." Hebrews 13:16

• **Let's read John 6:5-13 (as discussed in week three, day four).**

• **What was the disciple's first response to feeding ALL the people?**

_____

_____

• **What did Jesus do BEFORE he distributed the bread among the people?**

_____

_____

• **How much was left over from the five loaves of bread?**

_____

_____

We have to look back on an important lesson we learned in week one. The world tells us in order to believe, we need to **see** ... first. Jesus tells His disciples, and us, **we need to BELIEVE in order to SEE.** Jesus gave thanks BEFORE the miracle.

He believed God would work. He was a humble Servant who did not take **anything** for granted. He offered UP a sacrifice of PRAISE to God, the fruit of His lips, giving THANKS to His name. In obedience, He offered praise. The result? There was plenty left over, an abundance—beyond what they ever thought or imagined. That's what happens when thanksgiving is mixed with obedience. When we walk with unthankful hearts, we walk in pure selfishness. When we walk in obedience, **praise**, and service to others, we will walk in selflessness, thankfulness, and abundance.

• **What do the following verses say about walking with THANKFUL hearts? How are we to come before the Lord?**

• **Psalm 95:1-7**

_____

_____

• **Psalm 100:4-5**

_____

_____

• **Philippians 4:6**

_____

_____

We are to come—**thankful.**

In week nine of studying PLANTED, we should have LOTS of reasons to WALK in THANKFULNESS. It's not always easy, but we are called to do it. It's our sacrifice. It's our obedience. I have written in my Bible that if we do not walk with thankful hearts, it doesn't matter how obedient we are. Obedience flows from the appreciation of ALL that God is.

• **Let's close today by reading Psalm 89:15-16.**

The Message says:

> "Blessed are the people who know the **passwords of praise**,
> who shout on parade in the bright presence of God.
> Delighted, they dance all day long; they know
> who you are, what you do—they can't keep it quiet!
> Your vibrant beauty has gotten inside us—
> you've been so good to us! We're walking on air!
> All we are and have we owe to God,
> Holy God of Israel, our King!"

Psalm 89:15-16

"**Blessed** are those who have LEARNED to ACCLAIM you, who WALK in the light of your presence, Lord. They REJOICE in your name ALL day long; they CELEBRATE your righteousness."

Can you see the PRAISE? Can you hear the THANKSGIVING? Can you receive the GOOD NEWS? We can learn how to walk with God. Psalm 89 reminds us that it takes **practice.** It's not easy to acclaim Him when you are suffering, but we must. Thankfulness releases us from our bitterness, our walls of depression, and our selfishness. We must dig deep and remember WHO GOD IS during times of doubt and remember what HE HAS done for us in our lives. He is the I AM. He is WITH us. He will never leave us. He is faithful. He knew us before we were born. He calls us wonderful. We are His creation. We are His.

His desire is that we are **PLANTED** before Him, offering the praise and thanksgiving that ONLY HE deserves. Fellow tree, what are your **passports of PRAISE,** today? Are you dancing before Him? Has God's VIBRANT beauty been engraved into your root system so you can't help but praise Him?

Let's close today with this prayer:

Thank You Lord for You are good. I praise You Lord for You are Holy. You are grace, and You are my glory. I will trust in You. Help me, O Lord, and teach me to walk in Your ways. You are my strength, and in You I find rest. I want to be a tree PLANTED that ALWAYS lifts up her hands in praise to my King! Teach me to acclaim You. Amen.

• **Now it's your turn. What passports of PRAISE will you offer up today?**

_____

_____

_____

DAY FOUR/ WALK WITHOUT RUNNING

How do you **WALK**? I mean, do you have a certain gait or a particular strut? My Mom was nicknamed "duck" in college because they said she had a cute "waddle." (Still does by the way!) I know I walk a little "turned out" from all my ballet classes. Some of us are pigeon-toed and some of us walk straight and narrow. Some of us are fast walkers, some are slow walkers, some are speed walkers, and some of us need a walker!

We ALL have different **walks**. And I bet you can identify those closest to you because of the **distinct way** they walk. I can spot my children 500 yards away. My husband? A dead give away. How is this true? We decipher the way people walk, especially those who are closest to us, because we **know** them. We live with them. We saw our children take their first step. God sees us the same way. He knows our walk, He sees our steps, and still … **He chooses to walk with us.**

> **• Look up Leviticus 26:12 and identify the benefit of God walking with us.**

"I will WALK AMONG you and be YOUR God, and YOU WILL be my PEOPLE."

Leviticus 26:12

We are His people! We are daughters of the King! He does not leave our side. He walks with us, and He walks AMONG us.

> **• Why is WALK the verb of choice in this verse? Why not run? Why not jog? Why not limp along?**

_____

_____

Close your eyes and listen to the sound you hear at the pool in the summertime. WALK … DO NOT RUN! I can hear my Mom right now, "Annie, you're going to split your head wide-open!" Well, it happened. Not to me, but to my daughter, Winnie. We were at the pool, and it had just rained. The skies had cleared, but the cement around the pool was still slippery. She took one quick step from the grass to the cement and whoop! Up she went and down she fell. We ended up in the ER with a concussion. Praise God, she bounced right back (no pun intended).

When we run, we have a tendency to slip. To walk means … to walk. The dictionary on my computer says this:

> **WALK** means to: "move at a regular and fairly slow pace by lifting and setting down each foot in turn, never having both feet off the ground at once, archaic used to describe the way in which someone lives or behaves: walk humbly with your God." [3]

One of the main reasons I think God asks us to walk is so we can **hear** Him. When you are running, you can't really have a conversation about the most recent struggle in your life. At least, I can't. When you are walking, you can discuss what's on your heart. Walking is **communion**. Walking **bonds friendship** and brings us closer to one another. I have two friends with whom I try to walk with every Friday morning. I love this time. It's precious to me. Why? As we are walking together, we are sharing one another's pain, joy, love, fears, and hopes. Our walks are **purposeful.** We are not in a hurry to pass the time. We are simply enjoying each step.

This is another pivotal point I want us to learn today. Why are we in such a hurry? We live life in such a fast pace of "let's get this done," "I need this by tomorrow," "we are going to be late," and "there's not enough time in the day" mode. God just wants us to STOP and WALK with Him. Be patient. Be trusting. God has a reason in the walking … and waiting.

- **Let's take a look at how Jesus WALKED in John 11:1-7.**
  - **What is the situation?**

_____

_____

_____

  - **What does Jesus do in verse 6? Why? How many days have gone by when Jesus arrives?** _____

_____

_____

_____

This story is rich beyond measure. I encourage you to read John 1:1-44 to grasp the whole scene. Our focus today, though, is walking in **patience.** Why didn't Jesus run to Lazarus? Why didn't He send word that He was coming as fast as His earthly sandals could take Him?

  - **What are your thoughts?**

_____

_____

_____

We have an oncologist in our Sunday School class who loves Jewish history. Kevin explained that Jews believed a person's soul stayed with them for three days after death and then rose to the bosom of Abraham. For this reason, Jesus WAITED until the 4th day to raise Lazarus. After He had gotten word that Lazarus was sick, Jesus explained to His disciples that this sickness would not end in death, but to reveal God's glory. Jesus' raising of Lazarus from the dead after four days was yet another sign to prove to the people Jesus was in fact the Messiah. Perhaps another reason Jesus waited four days was so there would be no controversy that Lazarus was actually DEAD. Four days is good enough for me!

Jesus was patient in His steps because He **knew** God had a plan and a **purpose** for the wait. He **trusted** His father and **WALKED** into that faith.

  - **I saw a t-shirt that said, "Patience carries a lot of wait." Looking back in your life, can you see God's purpose in the waiting?**

_____

_____

God walks in the midst of us. He is **purposeful** with every step we take, and His desire is to commune with us. He knows life is slippery and sometimes we want to **rush** it. Take Him by the hand and trust Him. Take His lead and listen to His voice saying, "_____ (add your name), WALK don't run! You're going to split your head wide-open!"

Let's close with a quote from Sarah Young in _Jesus Calling._[4]

"Through the intimacy of our relationship, you are being transformed from the inside out. As you keep your focus on Me, I form you into the one I desire you to be. Your part is to yield to MY creative work in you, neither resisting it nor trying to speed it up. Enjoy the tempo of a God-breathed life by letting Me set the pace. Hold my hand in childlike trust, and the way before you will open up step by step."

Are we walking in childlike trust? Here's your assignment for today—**SLOW DOWN.** Walk at a pace where you can hear His voice. Enjoy both of your feet **on the ground.** It's certainly not archaic to WALK with God. Listen to His tempo, and let Him set the pace.

DAY FIVE/ WALKING IN CONFIDENCE

As I was checking out of Target yesterday, this thought occurred to me. In order for the automatic doors to open, I had to push my very overloaded cart right up to the point where the doors would open. I had to **believe with confidence** the doors would swing wide-open. These doors were not going to open while I was still at the checkout counter. I had to **walk right up** to them. I think God works like this sometimes, too. We have to believe and take action **all the way** to the edge of the opening of doors. Let me explain.

- **Open your Bibles and read Joshua 3:9-17.**

  - **When the Israelites crossed the Jordan, at what stage was the river?**

  _____

  _____

  - **What happened the second their feet touched the water?**

  _____

  _____

  - **Looking back at Joshua 3:5, what did Joshua tell the people?**

  _____

  _____

When the Israelites took steps of **confidence,** the waters from upstream **STOPPED flowing**, allowing them to cross into the Promised Land. Do you remember where they had been for 40 years? They were wandering in the desert. Why? Because they **weren't** so confident in the plans of the Lord. In fact, they were the opposite of confident—they were **unbelieving complainers!**

Read Numbers 32: 11-13.

> "'Because they have not followed me **wholeheartedly**, not one of the men twenty years old or more who came up out of Egypt will see the land I promised on oath to Abraham, Isaac and Jacob— not one except Caleb son of Jephunneh the Kenizzite and Joshua son of Nun, for they followed the Lord wholeheartedly.' The Lord's anger burned against Israel and he made them wander in the desert forty years, until the whole generation of those who had done evil in his sight was gone."

Notice what it says. They did not follow me _____.

The King James version says "they did not **wholly follow** me."

        Wholly means: full, to be filled, satisfy and **follow** is: behind, from following after.

In other words, the Israelites were not 100% behind following God. They were **not** confident in His provision. Wholeheartedly means complete **commitment** and complete **sincerity.** Because of their unbelief, God allowed them to wander.

Psalm 1:1 is an example of those who do not walk with God. They are walking with sinners, standing with mockers, and sitting with those who think a lot about themselves. Here, we see another example of those who chose their own way as well. Our walk needs to be different. Our walk needs to reflect **sincerity and commitment.** My mother always told me to be "lady-like." I am here to tell you today, that we need to be "tree-like!"

• **Notice what God tells Joshua in Joshua 1:6-9 before the Israelites cross over into the Promised Land.**

Does this sound familiar? I sure hope so! Prayerfully by now, after studying nine weeks of PLANTED, we should know we need to meditate on God's Truth day and night and be CAREFUL to do what is written in it. Then we shall be prosperous and successful. Our leaf will not wither, our fruit will yield in season, and whatever we do will prosper. We are a tree PLANTED, and GOD is WITH us. He has a plan for our lives. He goes behind us and before us. We have **confidence** in our King because of His overwhelming desire to **love** us. Period.

• **Take a look at these verses and let them soak into your root system. Grab some index cards and write them down. What do they say about walking in confidence? Who is our confidence?**

    • **Proverbs 3:26**

    _____

    _____

    • **Jeremiah 17:7-8**

       "But blessed is the man who trusts in the LORD, whose **confidence** is in him. He will be like a tree **planted** by the water that sends out its roots by the stream. It does not fear when heat comes; its leaves are always green. It has no worries in a year of drought and never fails to bear fruit."

    _____

    _____

    • **Ephesians 3:12**

       "In him and through faith in him we may approach God with freedom and **confidence.**"

    _____

    _____

    • **Hebrews 4:15-16**

    "For we do not have a high priest who is unable to sympathize with our weaknesses, but we have one who has been tempted in every way, just as we are--yet was without sin. Let us then approach the throne of grace with **confidence**, so that we may receive mercy and find grace to help us in our time of need."

    _____

    _____

    • **Isaiah 32:17**

    _____

    _____

When we walk with confidence in God, we can stand on these **promises**:

- God will keep us from stumbling.
- We will never fail to bear fruit … even in tough situations.
- We can always talk to Him and always come to Him with our cares and concerns.
- He will always be able to identify with our weakness.
- We will always find mercy, grace, peace, and rest.

- **Are you walking with confidence in the Lord? Are you 100% convinced of His goodness?**

- **What is keeping you from believing wholeheartedly? What is snaring you today? Tell Him.**

_____
_____
_____
_____
_____
_____
_____
_____

Jesus asked Martha, "**Do you believe**?" Read this account in John 11:21-27.

> "Lord," Martha said to Jesus, "**if** you had been here, my brother would not have died. But I know that even now God will give you whatever you ask." Jesus said to her,
> **"Your brother will rise again."**
> Martha answered, "I know he will rise again in the resurrection at the last day."
> Jesus said to her, "I am the resurrection and the life. The one who believes in me will live, even though they die; and whoever lives by believing in me will never die. **Do you believe this**?"
> "Yes, Lord," she replied, **"I believe** that you are the Messiah, the Son of God, who is to come into the world."

Notice Martha's first conversation with the Lord. **IF** you had been here, my brother would not have died. Have you ever used the word **IF** in your conversations with the Lord? **IF** I had not made that decision. **IF** I had not married so young. **IF** I had not taken this job … and so on. Does this resemble a confident faith or a haphazard belief? Is your walk with God on an "if" basis? Is it an "I'm happy as long as I am living in happy circumstances" basis? "I'll believe in God IF and when … ."

I am here to tell you that God does not operate this way. He says trust in Him **no matter what**. He is not a "vending machine God" that will only appear in your life IF it's going the way you planned. He's there. **Always.**

- **I love the example Jesus sets for us. Read John 11:38-44.**

I can hear Him saying, "Annie, did I not tell you that if you believed, you would **SEE** the glory of God." Do you think it's time you stepped into the river with **CONFIDENCE** believing the waters are going to stop flowing? The Promise Land is close. Take the **confident step** and believe. Whether it's an overloaded grocery cart or on overloaded heart, God wants you to take the first step to watch, to walk, to believe, and to **SEE the glory of God.**

"No need to panic over alarms or surprises, or predictions that doomsday's just around the corner, Because God will be **right there with you;** he'll keep you SAFE and SOUND."

Proverbs 3:26 (MSG)

VIEWER GUIDE: SESSION NINE
WALKING IN CONFIDENCE

WALKING INTO THE LIKENESS OF CHRIST.

1. We all have a different "walk," but the one thing we have in common is this:
- God wants our walk to be HUMBLE.
- He wants us to have complete _____.

When we are surrendered and humble, we can walk with CONFIDENCE into the purposes He has created for each of us.

Colossians 2:6-7
"So then, just as you have received Christ Jesus as Lord, continue to live in Him, rooted and built up in Him, strengthened in the faith as you were taught, and overflowing with thankfulness."

2. We have to WALK while being _____. Roots are our support system that store up the food of Scripture. This food is the LIVING Word sent out by God. It always produces fruit and prospers everywhere it is sent.

- Obedience is stepping into our FAITH; walking in _____.

3. We need to _____ on into that which Christ has taken hold of for us. We have to be established in our faith. It's easy to lead when your strong.

- Paul's goal was to KNOW Christ.
- Paul's goal was to KNOW the power of the resurrection.
- Paul's goal was to KNOW the fellowship of sharing in Christ's sufferings.

Are we living this life believing we have WON? It is by obedience alone that we PRESS ON toward the goal.

SPORTS HAVE RULES. SO DOES GOD.

Deuteronomy 10:12-13
"And now, Israel, what does the Lord your God ask of you but to FEAR the Lord your God, to WALK in obedience to Him, to LOVE Him, to SERVE the Lord your God with all your heart and with all your soul, and to observe the Lord's commandments and decrees that I am giving you today for your own good?"

- **Rules for following GOD:** Females Walk Low to Serve the KING.
  - F ~ **Fear** the Lord
  - W ~ **Walk** in all His ways
  - L ~ **Love** Him
  - S ~ **Serve** Him with all your heart and soul
  - K ~ **Keep** the Lord's commandments

"Blessed is the man who trusts me, God, the woman who sticks with God. They're like trees replanted in Eden, putting down roots near the rivers. Never a worry through the hottest of summers, never dropping a leaf, serene and calm through droughts, bearing fresh fruit every season."

Jeremiah 17:7-8 (MSG)

4. We have to WALK _____ Him, giving Him the THANKSGIVING! Always give Him your best.

   • Do you have this attitude of praising Him? Do you begin your day with thanksgiving?

When we praise God, there is _____. **Worship diffuses WORRY.**

5. Jesus IS the BREAD of Life. He taught the disciples to pray: Give us this day our daily BREAD.

When we come and SIT with the Living Bread, with a heart of THANKSGIVING and PRAISE, our time SPENT with Him will be MULTIPLIED not _____.

6. Sometimes it's hard to thank God for our situations. We are not praising the circumstance, but the ONE who _____ the circumstance. We can PRAISE God because we are focusing ON GOD not our circumstance.

7. Praising God takes _____. Praising God is a learning process as He teaches us to walk in the light of His presence.

What are your passports of praise? There is **POWER in the PRAISE**. Press on, my friend, press on. And DO YOUR BEST. Nothing is impossible with God! Amen.

NOTES:

WEEK TEN: DAY ONE/ WALKING IN STEP WITH THE SPIRIT

I am honestly amazed I just typed week TEN! The Lord has been so faithful to allow us this time to take the journey of PLANTED together. I pray you really **understand** what it means to SIT, STAND, and WALK in your faith with Jesus. We are blessed beyond imagination when we take the time to be with Him—whether we **have** the time or when we "think" we don't. Martin Luther once said, "I have so much to do today that I will spend the first three hours in prayer." [1] How much do you have to do today? Honestly, the more you have on your "plate," the MORE time you should make to SIT with God—first. Believe you me, I am the first guilty girl on the list. Rest assured, I am not pointing any fingers! I know from experience that when I take time to SIT, I am blessed to **STAND** on His promises, and to **WALK** in His purposes throughout my day.

- **What are some of the excuses you have for not having time to SIT?**
(especially doing Bible Studies around Christmas time … ouch!)

> "So I say, let the Holy Spirit GUIDE your lives. Then you won't be doing what your sinful nature craves."
>
> Galatians 5:16 (NLT)

We really have no excuse NOT to sit with the Lord. Why would we get up and run through the day on our own when He has promised to help us through it? He has promised to WALK with us, lead us, guide us, and pray for us. Let's take a deep breath today and ask Him to remind us to STOP.

This week we will look at **WALKING in the Spirit.** Walking in the Spirit reminds me of walking on the beach on a cool fall day. The sand is hard, the sun is out, the breeze is refreshing—**easy** and **delightful.** Sometimes though, it's HOT. Sweat starts to bead on your forehead, and it's hard to take the next step. The sand seems to sink, the future looks hazy—**trusting** and **believing.** Sometimes the beach turns overcast. Unexpected rain pours down and the sand is penetrated with raindrops—**sorrow** and **suffering.** The point is—we are called to WALK in the SPIRIT no matter what the forecast says. If we make the time to SIT with God before we head out on our walk, we can endure the sun, enjoy the breeze, and battle the rain. Grab your rain jacket of faith and bring along your water bottle for rehydration. We are about to **WALK** in the Spirit.

- **Let's begin by looking up Galatians 5:16-26.**
These verses are packed with GOOD "Spirit walking stuff." Let's take a seat and unpack this Scripture bit by bit.

- **According to Galatians 5:16-18, why should we live by the Spirit?**

_____

_____

- **Why is the sinful nature in conflict with the Spirit? (verses 16-18)**

_____

_____

- **List some of the acts of the sinful nature. Which ones are convicting to you? (verses 19-21)**

_____

_____

When we receive Jesus to be our Lord and Savior, we are sealed with the Holy Spirit. His Spirit comes to live WITH and IN us. We are free from the law of trying to please God by doing acts of goodness or kindness. Fortunately, there is no "brown-nosing" in the Kingdom of God. He loves us simply because **He sees Jesus in our hearts.** We are saved by His love and GRACE alone. This being true, we still battle with our sinful desires. We still battle with trying to please God or trying to be "good" enough to capture His attention. This is why it is SO IMPORTANT to wake up and SIT with the Lord before we start our day. Our sinful side has desires, too. Bring our desires to the river and washing them before the Lord is a great start to living by the Spirit.

We need to delight ourselves in Him—FIRST, then He will give us the DESIRES of our heart. We need to be bendable and moldable like the limber pine. When we walk through our day without giving a bending ear to the Lord, we walk in our own selfishness. Yuck.

We should walk in the good 'ole FRUIT of the Spirit. When we are PLANTED by streams of water, our FRUIT will yield in season. The fruit of "love, joy, peace, patience, kindness, goodness, faithfulness, gentleness, and self-control" will be evident in our lives. Yeah.

- **Let's read again Galatians 5:22-26.**

  - **Why is there no law against such things? (verse 23)**

    _____

    _____

  - **What is our promise of belonging to the Lord? (verse 24)**

    _____

    _____

  - **Finish these two sentences. (verse 25)**

    Let us: _____

    Let us NOT: _____

The law was given in the Old Testament to reveal sin. But Galatians reminds us that if we belong to Christ, He has crucified the sinful nature in us with its passions and desires. Jesus gives us a new heart with new desires that please God. We are no longer under the law of sin because Jesus demolished the power of the sin nature in us when He died on the cross. We are now being filled with the fruit of the Spirit when we choose to WALK in His ways.

I love my friend's analogy that walking in the Spirit is like walking around with "fruity bubble wrap!" I guess it's the modern-day armor of God. When we keep in step with the Spirit, our sinful desires just bounce right off.

Are you fearing something today? … **boing** … Keeping in step with the Spirit means trusting in God's unfailing love (Psalm 13:5-6). Are you jealous of someone? … **boing** … Keeping in step means being happy with their success. Are you guilty of quick anger? … **boing** … Keep in step with patience and self-control. Are you depressed? … **boing** … Keep in step with God's faithfulness, gentleness, and peace.

- **I want to close today by reading Psalm 121 and end with a personal prayer.**
  While reading, be mindful of walking **in step** with the Spirit.

> "I lift up my eyes to the hills. From where does my help come?
> My help comes from the Lord, who made heaven and earth.
> He will not let your foot be moved; he who keeps you will not slumber.
> Behold, he who keeps Israel will neither slumber nor sleep.
> The Lord is your keeper; the Lord is your shade on your right hand.
> The sun shall not strike you by day, nor the moon by night.
> The Lord will keep you from all evil; he will keep your life.
> The Lord will keep your going out and your coming in from this time forth and forevermore."

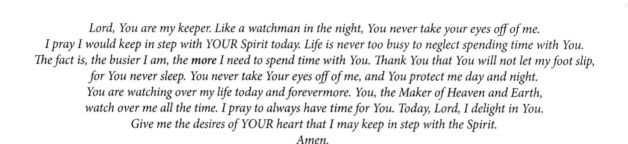

Lord, You are my keeper. Like a watchman in the night, You never take your eyes off of me.
I pray I would keep in step with YOUR Spirit today. Life is never too busy to neglect spending time with You.
*The fact is, the busier I am, the **more** I need to spend time with You. Thank You that You will not let my foot slip,*
for You never sleep. You never take Your eyes off of me, and You protect me day and night.
You are watching over my life today and forevermore. You, the Maker of Heaven and Earth,
watch over me all the time. I pray to always have time for You. Today, Lord, I delight in You.
Give me the desires of YOUR heart that I may keep in step with the Spirit.
Amen.

DAY TWO/ I WANT TO BE LIKE YOU

As I began writing this morning, I couldn't get the song from the old *Jungle Book* movie out of my mind! Remember when the monkey was singing with Mowgli … "I want to be like you?"

> "Oh, oobee doo
> I wanna be like you
> I wanna walk like you
> I wanna talk like you
>
> You'll see it's true
> Someone like me
> Can learn to be
> Like someone like you"
> The Jungle Book [2]

Are you starting to hum the tune? I want to be more like Jesus. How about you? Do you want to talk like Him? Do you want to WALK like Him? Even someone like you and me can learn to be someone like Him! This is why we MUST keep in STEP with the Spirit. Today, we are going to study how to learn to WALK in **forgiveness**.

- **What do the following verses teach us about forgiveness?**

  - **Ephesians 4:32**

  _____

  _____

  - **1 Peter 3:8-12**

  _____

  _____

  - **Colossians 2:13-15**

  _____

  _____

After reading these Scriptures, I can hear myself repeating the following phrases to my children over and over again.

Curry, please try to get along! Winnie, you need to forgive her and yourself. John, don't hold a grudge. Daley, put down your phone and take a deep breath. Do NOT text back. Jesus forgave you, so you need to forgive. You need to be a blessing in order to receive a blessing.

This is basic mom intervention. But forgiveness is A LOT harder when the offenses go outside of your parental jurisdiction. Have you ever had these conversations with the Lord before?

Lord, You are asking me not to retaliate? Are You kidding? Did You see what he did to me?
Lord, You are asking me to forgive her? Maybe You were sleeping. Did You hear how her words hurt?
Lord, You are asking me to be calm? Are You for real? Did You notice the _____.

Forgiveness can be one of the hardest things required of us as a believer. Why? Because everything in our sinful character wants to contradict the Spirit inside of us. We want revenge. We want justice. We must remind ourselves that we are a tree **PLANTED**—especially for times like these. Are we trusting the Living Water inside of us to cool down our emotions? Do we have the faith to forgive others as well as ourselves? Do we really want to be like Jesus? Do we really want to walk like Him and talk like Him?

Romans 12:19 says:

"Do not take revenge, my dear friends, but leave room for God's wrath, for it is written: 'It is mine to avenge; I will repay,' says the Lord."

God is a just God, and it is His job to avenge. Our job is to trust and forgive as Jesus forgave us.

- **What do these two verses say about allowing God to take care of things?**

  - **Hebrews 12:14**

    _____

    _____

  - **1 Peter 3:9**

    _____

    _____

It's hard. That's why Paul says MAKE EVERY EFFORT, do not repay evil with evil, but instead, **bless**. Not in your own strength, but in the strength of Christ. Here's another big reason. When we surrender our jurisdiction of justification, others will SEE THE LORD. We are different. We stand out. We are trees **PLANTED**. It's not natural to forgive. So why do we do it? Because Jesus forgave our sin to set us free from the law of sin and death (Romans 8:1-2). He forgave us so we would have the power to forgive others and point them to the ONE who set us free.

Look at the examples of Jesus.

"He did not retaliate when he was insulted, nor threaten revenge when he suffered. He left his case in the hands of God, who always judges fairly." 1 Peter 2:23 (NLT)
"Jesus said, 'Father, forgive them, for they do not know what they are doing.'
And they divided up his clothes by casting lots." Luke 23:34

"Summing up:
Be agreeable,
be sympathetic,
be loving,
be compassionate,
be humble.
That goes for ALL of
you, no
exceptions.
No retaliation. No
sharp-tongued
sarcasm.
Instead, BLESS—that's
your job,
to BLESS. You'll be a
BLESSING and also get
a BLESSING."

1 Peter 3:8-12
(MSG)

We need to be like HIM.

I think the monkey had it right. We have to LEARN to be like Jesus. It takes **time**. It takes **faith**. It takes **walking in the Spirit**. Oh, oobee doo.

> "BLESSED are those who have LEARNED to acclaim you,
> who WALK in the light of your presence, O LORD."
>
> Psalm 89:15

DAY THREE/ THE THREE "C's"

When I think about **walking** in the Spirit, I think about something my mentor shared with me years ago, "Annie, be careful about the three 'C's,—**Complaining, Controlling, and Comparing.**" Just as Psalm 1 opens with "*Blessed are those who do NOT, … .*" I believe the same is true with keeping in step with the Spirit. Blessed are those who do NOT … **Complain, Control, and Compare**. If you are ever wondering if you are IN or OUT of sync with the Spirit, just ask yourself, "Am I complaining? Am I controlling? Am I comparing?"

Let's look at **COMPLAINING** first. Yes, I know, this day could sting a bit.

> • **Read Philippians 2:14-16.**
>
>> • **For what reason should we not complain or argue?**
>>
>> _____
>> _____
>>
>> • **What is the promise when we do not give in to this desire?**
>>
>> _____
>> _____

Notice there is not an "exception" policy. Do EVERYTHING without complaining: except when you lose your job, your children are driving you CRAZY, it's *that* time of month, you are tired, you have the flu, or you _____.

"Lord," you may say, "How can I possibly **not** complain when_____has happened?" Remember to **remember** (week five, day four). Let's remember what we have learned.

> • **Read Romans 12:17. What does the Holy Spirit enable us to do?**
>
> _____
> _____
>
> • **What does Romans 12:12 say about the subject?**
>
> _____
> _____

Our GOAL is to **WALK in the Spirit.**

> The Spirit gives us the **POWER** to overcome evil.
> The Spirit gives us the **POWER** to overcome complaining.
> We can be **joyful** in hope because Jesus **is** our Hope.
> We can be **patient** in affliction because God promises us that as HIS children and believers in Christ, He will cause everything to work together for GOOD.
> We can be **faithful** in prayer because HE alone is faithful.

"And we KNOW that God causes EVERYTHING to work TOGETHER for the GOOD of those who LOVE God and are CALLED according to HIS purpose for them."

Romans 8:28 (NLT)

• What about **CONTROLLING**—the second deadly "C?" What happens when we try to control?

When my son, Curry, was two years old, I looked at him one day and his left eye was smack dab **stuck** in the corner. His eye was permanently crossed. With the normal alarm of any parent, we got an appointment to see a specialist. They requested an MRI the next day. The only rules given were no food, no drink, no nothing. Well, they did say he could have a popsicle.

As a good mom, I went to the store and got him a Scooby-Doo Push-Up™. As I was driving to the Children's Hospital, the thought occurred to me, *"Annie, did you realize you gave your son a PUSH-UP and not a POPSICLE! There is milk in a push-up, Annie. He can't have milk!"*

I kept quiet until Curry was called back into the pre-surgery room. By this time, my guilt was growing heavier and heavier. The kind nurse turned "monster on me" when I finally and painfully pushed out the words, "I gave him a **p-u-s-h-u-p** not a **p-o-p-s-i-c-l-e.**" She immediately called headquarters and briskly told me that he could **not** have the MRI. It would be another two weeks before they could see him again.

MY FAULT.

My little boy had to wait two more weeks without a result because of ME. My **"CONTROL-mode"** kicked in. Instead of trusting the matter to God, I racked my brain as to who I could "call" to get him in sooner. Who did I "know?" Whose name could I drop? I was devastated and humiliated. And I was not about to forgive myself. Down I went on the roller coaster of "what-if." What if he had a brain tumor? What if I had not given him the push-up? What if, what if, **what if?**

My sweet husband stopped the bleeding when he looked at me with tenderness and said, "It's ok, Annie—maybe you gave up Curry's spot to allow another child to have an MRI who really needed a diagnosis."

Who demonstrated faith? My husband surrendered **control** and met me with **compassion**. Me? I was the CONTROL FREAK. Lesson? GIVE up the Control. We are powerless anyway.

Let's be reminded of these verses and take **comfort.**

• **Psalm 55:22**

> *"GIVE your burdens to the LORD, and he will take care of you.
> He will not permit the godly to slip and fall." (NLT)*

• **Psalm 3:5-6**

> *"Trust in the Lord with all your heart and lean NOT on your own understanding;
> in ALL your ways submit to him, and he will make your paths STRAIGHT."*

Last but not least, let's look at **COMPARING**.

Comparing is one of Satan's oldest tools in the shed. When we compare ourselves with others, we slip down the slide thinking God isn't good enough. When we start down this slippery slope, we begin to believe God doesn't really care about us. This is DANGEROUS territory. We need some good "roto-**root**ering." (PLANTED pun intended.) We need to flush out the bad and be filled with the good —the goodness of God. Bad roots can destroy a tree in no time.

The Message says that by comparing ourselves with others, we are totally **MISSING the POINT.** Read 2 Corinthians 10:12 in the left column.

- **What do the following verses tell us about God's love for us?**

- **Matthew 7:7-8**

_____

_____

- **Matthew 10:29-31**

_____

_____

- **Romans 8:28**

_____

_____

- **Psalm 84:11**

> "For the LORD God is a sun and shield: the LORD will give grace and glory:
> no good thing will he withhold from them that walk uprightly."

_____

_____

- **Jeremiah 17:7-10**

> "Blessed is the man that trusteth in the LORD, and whose HOPE the LORD is.
> For he shall be as a tree PLANTED by the waters, and that spreadeth out her roots by the river,
> and shall not see when heat cometh, but her leaf shall be GREEN;
> and shall not be careful in the year of drought,
> neither shall cease from yielding fruit."

_____

_____

Let's not miss the POINT. Playing the comparing game is senseless. GOD loves us ALL—the same. Just as there is no "brown-nosing" in Heaven, there is no favoritism either. God has a purpose for each of us and equips us equally with different gifts meant to glorify Him. We are not made to **complain, control, or compare.** We are made to be His beloved daughters who **TRUST** in the King's goodness. Our Father knows every hair on our head. He knows our mistakes, and He even knows when the next MRI is scheduled. He works out our situations for **GOOD,** and He will withhold NO GOOD THING. It's a promise. WALK INTO IT.

Little Curry? He's now 13-years-old and has 20/20 vision. I will never know what child might have gotten his spot that day, but God does. Yes, He does work everything together for good. We are reminded of this every time we eat a Scooby-Doo P-U-S-H-up™ and not a P-O-P-sicle.

DAY FOUR/ GOIN' AND NOT KNOWIN'

What happens when we are faithfully walking with the Lord, being obedient in our steps, but we can't see the road ahead, and we feel like we are "walking" in place?

Let me share a story with you. It's called *The Man by the Window*, by Harry Buschman.[3]

There were two men who shared a hospital room. The bed occupied by Mr. Vincent was placed by a window, while the other man, Mr. Parker, was confined to lying on his back due to a spinal injury. Each day, Mr. Vincent would sit up and relay to his bunkmate all the happenings of the world. Mr. Vincent became Mr. Parker's "eyes" to see what he could not. He told him about the sunshine, the children playing in the park, the lovers walking, the rippling of the lake, and the parade moving down the street. He described colors, noises, imagined smells, and told stories of onlookers. These stories would sustain the two men, giving them hope beyond the four walls of the gloomy hospital room. One day, the man next to the window died, and Mr. Parker asked to be moved … next to the window.

With a pause, the nurse replied, "Darling, there is no window. Just a brick wall."

> • **Do you ever feel this way? Do you ever feel that life is like staring at a brick wall, or do you see the windows of opportunity around every turn?**

Ephesians 5 tells us we need to be **imitators** of God and WALK in LOVE just as Christ did for us. This chapter in Ephesians reminds us to be a fragrant aroma as we discussed in week six, day three. It warns us against immorality and filthy talk and reminds us that we are **light in the LORD.** Fellow trees, we need to WALK as children of the LIGHT, making the most out of what has been so graciously given to us.

> • **Read Ephesians 5:8-16. What does verse 16 specifically tell us?**

_____

_____

We need to make the MOST of every opportunity—just like Mr. Vincent. There was no window, so why would he go to the effort to give hope to Mr. Parker? Mr. Vincent was imitating Christ. He was filling the hospital room with the fragrant aroma of love. True, there was not a window. Did this stop him from believing in hope? Did this stop him from being thankful? Did this stop him from loving his neighbor as himself?

> • **Read Psalm 46:4. How do you think a river can bring JOY?**

_____

_____

_____

_____

As I was researching this verse, I was amazed again. Read this footnote written in the NIV Study Bible, and sit in **awe** of God's Word.

"Jerusalem had no river, unlike Thebes, Damascus, Nineveh, or Babylon, yet she had a 'river.' Here the river serves as a metaphor for the continual outpouring of the sustaining and refreshing blessings of God, which make the city of God like the Garden of Eden."[4]

"A RIVER brings JOY to the city of our God, the sacred home of the Most High."

Psalm 46:4 (NLT)

Jerusalem had no river. The hospital room had no window. Do you ever feel there is no hope?

The Bible tell us to make the **MOST** of every opportunity (Colossians 4:5). Life is a gift. Although it is true we can do nothing in our own strength, we must remember we are connected to the Vine. We sit by the river every morning to be PLANTED for the day. There is promise. There is a **RIVER in JERUSALEM!** His name is JESUS, and He came to rescue you and me. We are PLANTED by this very stream and from this Source, we receive light and life. Without this connection, we are living in a room with four walls and no view.

• Where is the river in your life—the continual outpouring of the BLESSINGS of God?

_____

_____

_____

"Send forth your LIGHT and your TRUTH, let them GUIDE me; let them BRING me to YOUR holy mountain, to the place where YOU dwell."

Psalm 43:3

Philippians 2:15,16 reminds us that as we **walk** out our faith in the Lord, keeping in STEP with the Spirit:

> "… we will SHINE among them like STARS in the sky
> as [we] hold firmly to the word of life."

As we hold firmly to God's Word, as we meditate and delight in His Word, we will **SHINE.**

• Read Psalm 43:3. What does this say about God's light?

_____

_____

_____

Today, let's be obedient to **WALK**—even when there is not a "window" in sight. We need to light up God's kingdom with hope and love and fragrance. We need to have faith, even when we can't see out the window. Hebrews 11:1 tells us:

> "Faith is being SURE of what we HOPE for and CERTAIN of what we do not see."

Have you ever seen trees at Christmas time that are decorated with lights? It's almost magical. Let's be this tree today— lighting up the sky like stars as we hold firmly to the hand of God. He's leading. Would you like to take a walk in the light of FAITH today?

We need to **walk** as children of the light. We need to **shine** in the darkness of this world. We need to **bring** others into His presence. He is the source. Without Him, life is just another brick wall.

DAY FIVE/ WALKING IN VICTORY!

Wow! Today we are taking our last walk in **PLANTED** together. I can't even begin to express to you how this journey has strengthened my root system. I am praying you have grown as well—O, strong and mighty tree. What a privilege and a joy it has been to serve you!

Today, we are **walking in VICTORY**—not only in the Lord, but in celebration that we have studied TEN weeks together!

We started **PLANTED** by learning that God's ways are counter-cultural to the world's way. We saw in the first Psalm that the person who is not being blessed has her positioning all wrong. She is walking in wicked ways with selfish motives, standing with the wrong crowd, and sitting in poor choices. The woman who is blessed SITS **first** in the presence of the Lord. From here, she can STAND on His promises and WALK through her day with purpose.

> • **The first chapter of James is the perfect way to begin today's lesson. Can you find the three positions (in order) of sitting, standing, and walking?**
>
> > • **Look at James 1:5. For what is this person asking the Lord?**
> >
> > _____
> >
> > _____
> >
> > • **In James 1:6, what key STANDING position does this person have to take?**
> >
> > _____
> >
> > _____
> >
> > • **From James 1:22-25, how does this person have to WALK?**
> >
> > _____
> >
> > _____

The **first stance** is SITTING and asking the Lord for **wisdom**. We have mentioned that Psalm 139:23-24 is a good place to start our day. This asking and searching is the delighting and the meditating by the stream of water. Jesus is our source of water, and we need to take time to sit and soak up His wisdom. Without His wisdom, we are walking in our own flesh with no direction.

The **second stance** is STANDING on a strong BELIEF system and not doubting the Word of God. Our time spent sitting and being filled with the Holy Spirit enables us to stand on the Word that leads us and directs us through our day. If we begin to doubt, we are like a wave tossed by the sea—as my Mom says, "We are being 'wishy-washy.'"

The **third stance** is WALKING and DOING what God's Word says. Our roots have to be strong, our branches flexible, and our hearts filled to overflowing with the source of Spirit.

I have a sweet friend named Mary Glenn Peeples. She asked me one day, "Annie, what is God's **WILL** for you?" I replied with confidence, "To glorify Him in all that I say and do!" She sweetly said, "Nope."

> • **Let's look at Ephesians 5:17-20. What do you think God's will is for you?**
>
> _____
>
> _____

> "SEARCH me,
> God, and KNOW
> my heart;
> TEST me and
> know my anxious
> thoughts.
> See if there is
> ANY offensive way
> in me,
> and LEAD me in
> the WAY everlasting."
>
> Psalm 139:23-24

Yes! It's being filled with the Spirit. When we are filled, then we are **IN STEP.** We are alive to Christ and dead to our own desires.

She then asked, "Annie, what's God's **PURPOSE** for you?" I replied with less confidence, "To glorify Him in all that I say and do?" She said, "Nope."

• **Let's look up Romans 8:28-29. What do you think God's purpose is for you?**

_____

_____

Yes! It's to be like Jesus. To walk like Him and talk like Him. Do you remember the _Jungle Book_ song? Our purpose is to become more and more like-minded with Christ.

Finally she asked me, "Annie, what is God's plan for you? Without hesitation, I said, "I have NO IDEA!" She said, "To glorify Him in all that you say and do!"

We are to walk in the Spirit and imitate Jesus. We are to become trees with Christ-like fragrance glorifying Him in everything we say and do. We have discussed that we are His masterpiece, and we have been created to do good works. I love _The Message's_ translation of 1 Corinthians 12:7 and Ephesians 2:10.

"Each person is given something to DO to SHOW who God is."
1 Corinthians 12:7

"He creates each of us by Christ Jesus to JOIN HIM in the work He does, the good work he has gotten ready for us to do—the work we had better be doing."
Ephesians 2:10

Are we doing the work God has called us to do? Are we joining Him in the work He does? Max Lucado says we have all been given an "assignment." [5]

• **What's your assignment as you WALK with Christ?**

_____

_____

JESUS DIED ON A TREE

_____
FOR A TREE

Whatever your assignment looks like, you need to have the confidence to walk in **VICTORY**.

• **Let's read 1 Peter 2:23-25. According to this verse, what is the reason we can we walk in VICTORY?**

_____

_____

_____

_____

We can WALK in victory because Jesus Christ died on a tree for a tree—for you and me. He conquered sin and death so we may live for righteousness. By His suffering, we have been healed from eternal separation and have been returned to our rightful Lord, our Shepherd who oversees our lives.

Victory, you bet! Read this next verse … I have been waiting **ten weeks** to share it with you.

• **Please read Revelation 22:1-6.**

- **What is flowing from the throne of God and of the Lamb?**

_____

_____

- **What stood on each side of the river?**

_____

_____

I am not a "Revelation" scholar by any terms, but I believe this tree of life is the **same tree** that was in the Garden of Eden. While we are still living on earth, we have the choice each day to be "re-planted" in Eden through our delighting and meditating on God's Word (week two, day two). We have the **choice** to be strong trees that are **PLANTED** by the source of LIFE, so our fruit will yield in season, our leaf will not wither, and we will prosper in all we do. We have **the choice to WALK in the Victory of Jesus**—every day. Here's the future hope, the promise. One day, we will stand and see God face-to-face. We will SEE THE RIVER that is flowing from His throne. We will SEE THE TREE of LIFE that is yielding fruit every month. We will serve Him. There will be no more pain, crying, suffering, or loss. We will be with Him forever and ever.

I will close our study with this story: **The Texas Two-Step.**

When I lived in Dallas, one of the first things I learned was the "Two-Step." We went dancing one night when a **true** cowboy asked me to dance. When I say "true," I mean the whole nine-yards—ropers, wrangler jeans, and even an authentic cowboy hat. (Being from Florida, I was looking for his horse tied up out back!) Before I write anymore, you must know something about the two-step. If you don't know it, you are in big Texas trouble … especially when you hit the dance floor. It's a swirl of motion. You either go with the flow or get trampled. This cowboy knew the dance. He took the lead, and we swirled. His lead was strong and rhythmic. He knew the step, he knew the beat, and we danced with grace and ease.

God is like this cowboy in many ways. When we are in step with His Spirit, we are dancing with grace and ease, too. When life gets anxious, worrisome, tired, and weary, we are on the dance floor going in the wrong direction. We might not get trampled, but we will get hurt. Trust in the Lord. **PLANT** yourself right by His river every morning and be filled with the Spirit. **STAND** on His promises. **Walk** in His purposes. Take His hand, step out in faith, and BELIEVE. Don't doubt His lead, He's the real thing. By the way, this Cowboy has a horse called Faithful and True. He's waiting out back to ride us into eternity where He will reign forever.

I will close our study by praying Psalm 46 over us.

O Lord, we praise You for You are our refuge and our strength. We will not fear when life turns upside down because You have promised us that ALL things work together for the GOOD of those who love You. Lord, we love You. There is a river, Lord, one that makes GLAD the city of God. Father, we choose to come to this river each morning to be like a tree PLANTED. We come to this holy place to worship, meditate, and delight in You. You, Lord, are WITH us. We are Your Masterpiece, and You have given us each an assignment to be used to bring You glory. When we are still, we know YOU alone are God. You are exalted above the nations. You are exalted above the earth. I pray, today, we would be filled with Your Holy Spirit that we would become more and more like Your Son, Jesus Christ. Fill us with the Fruit of Your Spirit so we will SHINE like stars as we hold out the WORD of the Lord. Grow us into beautiful TREES that honor and glorify You. To You be the honor and the glory, forever and ever. Help us to be, PLANTED. Amen.

"Then the angel showed me the RIVER of the water of LIFE. It was as clear as glass and came from the throne of God and of the Lamb. It runs down the center of the street in the city. On each side of the river was the TREE of life. It gives twelve different kinds of FRUIT. It gives this fruit twelve times a year, NEW fruit each month. Its leaves are used to heal the nations. There will be NOTHING in the city that is sinful. The place where God and the Lamb SIT will be there. The servants He owns will serve Him. They will SEE His face and His name will be written on their foreheads. There will be no night there. There will be no need for a light or for the sun. Because the Lord God will be their light. They will be leaders forever."

Revelation 22:1-5
(NLT)

VIEWER GUIDE: SESSION TEN
WALKING STEP-BY-STEP IN THE SPIRIT

"So I say, walk by the Spirit, and you will not gratify the desires of the flesh. For the flesh desires what is contrary to the Spirit, and the Spirit what is contrary to the flesh. They are in conflict with each other, so that you are not to do whatever you want."

Galatians 5:16-17

We made it to the last teaching lesson! Do you see TREES differently? I sure hope so!

PLANTED: Sitting, Standing, and Walking with Jesus.

What is God's will for us? What is God's purpose for us? What is God's plan for us?

1. God's will for us is to walk in the power of the _____ _____.

   • **We need to walk with WISDOM.**
   • **We need to walk making the MOST of every opportunity.**
   • **We need to walk carefully.**
   • **We need to walk FILLED with the Holy Spirit.**

2. God teaches us step-by-step. We don't have to be embarrassed that we do not know the WHOLE Bible.

   5 P's for having a QUIET TIME: Priscilla Shirer, *Going Beyond Ministries*
   (http://www.goingbeyond.com/sites/default/files/content/CanWeTalk_Leader.pdf)

   * Position yourself to _____ from God.
   * Pour over the _____ and paraphrase the main points.
   * Pull out the spiritual _____.
   * Pose questions.
   * Plan obedience and pin down a date.

1 Corinthians 15:58
"Therefore, my dear brothers and sisters, stand firm. Let nothing move you. Always give yourselves fully to the work of the Lord, because you know that your labor in the Lord is not in vain."

3. Ask questions.

   • What moves you?
   • Do you ALWAYS give yourself fully to the Lord?

4. Look up one word at a time (blueletterbible.com). For example:

   • Fully means: to be over, to remain, to exceed a number of measure, to abound.
   • Abounding (fully) is used of a FLOWER going from bud to FULL-BLOOM. Now that is some PLANTED imagery!

5. Put a personal application to your verse. Ask God to remind you of a certain situation or story that parallels the Scripture.

What is the HOLY SPIRIT?

6. The first step is **confession** ~ a belief in Jesus Christ. Once we believe, the Holy Spirit seals us as His own. We are His children. But it is our _____ if we want to WALK with the Holy SPIRIT.

       We can either CONCEAL it, or REVEAL it. RECEIVE it, or GRIEVE it.
       Our flesh and our spirit are in conflict with each other.

7. When we WALK in the Spirit there is _____.

       • Our flesh wants to compare, control, and complain.
       • Our spirit invites love, joy, peace, and patience.
       • Our spirit wants to be more and more like Christ; to conform to His image.

8. Giving THANKS has POWER; it diffuses the power of the sinful nature. The HOLY SPIRIT has _____.

• The Holy Spirit can change us where we are able to forgive, to fight the battles of selfish desires, and to remain PLANTED.

Psalm 46:4
"There is a river whose streams make glad the city of God. The holy place where the Most High dwells."

9. We often can't SEE the river, but we have the power of the Holy Spirit in us to guide us. The Holy Spirit is continually pouring out Himself into our hearts. We have the VICTORY. Let's SIT, STAND, and WALK in the POWER of Jesus. Amen.

NOTES:

Notes:

CHAPTER ONE:
1. Stomie Omartian, *The Power of a Praying Wife*, (Eugene, Oregon, Harvest House Publishers, 1997).
2. Rick Warren, *40 Days in the Word*, (Rancho Santa Margarita, California, Sadleback Resources, 2011), pg. vi.
3. Sabbatismos: http://www.blueletterbible.org/lang/lexicon/lexicon.cfm?Strongs=G4520&t=KJV.
4. Definition of renew: http://www.blueletterbible.org/lang/lexicon/lexicon.cfm?Strongs=G342&t=KJV.
5. Corrie Ten Boom, http://www.goodreads.com/quotes/32394-if-you-look-at-the-world-you-ll-be-distressed-if.
6. Cloverton, *Take Me Into The Beautiful*, http://www.clovertonmusic.com.
7. Steven Curtis Chapman, *Dive*, © Universal Music Publishing Group, EMI Music Publishing.

CHAPTER TWO:
1. Definition of humph: http://www.merriam-webster.com/dictionary/humph.
2. Anapauō: http://www.blueletterbible.org/lang/lexicon/lexicon.cfm?Strongs=G373&t=KJV.
3. Anapausis: http://www.blueletterbible.org/lang/lexicon/lexicon.cfm?Strongs=G372&t=KJV.
4. Definition of humility: Merriam~Webster, http://www.merriam-webster.com/dictionary/humility, and The Free Dictionary, http://www.thefreedictionary.com/humility.
5. Tapeinoō: http://www.blueletterbible.org/lang/lexicon/lexicon.cfm?Strongs=G5013&t=KJV.
6. Lysa TerKeurst, *More Than a Good Bible Study Girl*, ©2009 Lysa TerKeurst; (P)2009 Zondervan, pg. 156-157.
7. Horatio G. Spafford, *It is Well With My Soul*, 1873.
8. Sam McBratney, *Guess How Much I Love You*, Candlewick Press, 2008.
9. Darash: http://www.biblestudytools.com/lexicons/hebrew/nas/darash.html.
10. Definition of blessed: http://www.merriam-webster.com/dictionary/blessed.

CHAPTER THREE:
1. New International Version Study Bible, Zondervan, Footnote: pg. 9.
2. Definition of put: http://www.merriam-webster.com/dictionary/put.
3. Sarah Young, *Jesus Calling*, (Nashville, Tennessee, Thomas Nelson Publishing, ©2004), August 29th, pg. 252.
4. Thayer's Lexicon, http://www.blueletterbible.org/lang/lexicon/lexicon.cfm?Strongs=G4049&t=KJV.
5. Arthur Tappan Pierson, *Steams in the Desert*, (Grand Rapids, Michigan, Zondervan, Copyright 1925), pg. 407.
6. Definition of sit: http://www.merriam-webster.com/dictionary/sit.

CHAPTER FOUR:
1. Charles Swindoll, http://www.goodreads.com/author/quotes/5139.Charles_R_Swindoll.
2. Definition of discretion: http://www.blueletterbible.org/lang/lexicon/lexicon.cfm?Strongs=H7922&t=KJV, Definition of slow: http://www.blueletterbible.org/lang/lexicon/lexicon.cfm?Strongs=H748&t=KJV, http://www.thefreedictionar com/slow, Definition of anger: http://www.blueletterbible.org/lang/lexicon/lexicon.cfm?Strongs=H639&t=KJV.
3. Definition of overlook: http://www.blueletterbible.org/lang/lexicon/lexicon.cfm?Strongs=H5674&t=KJV.
4. Samuel Dickey Gordon, *Streams in the Desert*, (Grand Rapids, Michigan, Zondervan, Copyright 1925), August 16, *pg. 313.*
5. Samuel Dickey Gordon, J.R. Miller, *Streams in the Desert*, (Grand Rapids, Michigan, Zondervan, Copyright 1925), August 16, pg. 313-314.
6. Steven Curtis Chapman, *Let us Pray*, Signs of Life, 1996.
7. George Mueller, http://christian-quotes.ochristian.com/George-Mueller-Quotes/page-3.shtml.
8. ThouArtExalted, www.thouartexalted.com.
9. Sarah Young, *Jesus Calling*, (Nashville, Tennessee, Thomas Nelson Publishing, ©2004), August 20th, pg. 243.

CHAPTER FIVE:
1. Definition of stand: http://www.thefreedictionary.com/stand.
2. Barbara Brown Taylor, *Altar in the World*, http://www.goodreads.com/work/quotes/5833971-an-altar-in-the-world-a-geography-of-faith.
3. A. B. Simpson, *Streams in the Desert*, (Grand Rapids, Michigan, Zondervan, Copyright 1925), September 9th, pg. 344.
4. Bob Goff, *Love Does*, (Nashville, Tennessee, Thomas Nelson, 2012), pg. 174.
5. Brandon Heath, *Jesus in Disguise*, Mountain.
6. Charles Spurgeon, *Streams in the Desert*, (Grand Rapids, Michigan, Zondervan, Copyright 1925), August 30th, pg. 333.
7. http://txforestservice.tamu.edu/main/popup.aspx?id=1283.
8. Henry J. van Dyke, *Joyful, Joyful, We Adore Thee*, 1907.

CHAPTER SIX:
1. Rick Warren, *40 Days in the Word*, (Rancho Santa Margarita, California, Sadleback Resources, 2011), pg. 2.
2. Dr. Charles Stanley, excerpted from "*The Power Within*" by In Touch Ministries, http://www.jesus.org/following-jesus/ fruit of-the-spirit/how-does-the-holy-spirt-empower-believers.html.
3. NIV Study Bible, Zondervan, Footnote: pg. 1765.
4. Greg Laurie, http://www.jesus.org/following-jesus/fruit-of-the-spirit/how-do-we-bear-spiritual-fruit.html.
5. Austin Phelps, *Streams in the Desert*, (Grand Rapids, Michigan, Zondervan, Copyright 1925) *pg. 449.*
6. Definition of fruitful: http://www.thefreedictionary.com/fruitful.

CHAPTER SEVEN:
1. Anag: http://www.blueletterbible.org/lang/lexicon/lexicon.cfm?Strongs=H6026&t=KJV.
2. Nathan: http://www.blueletterbible.org/lang/lexicon/lexicon.cfm?Strongs=H5414&t=KJV.
3. New International Version Study Bible, Zondervan, Footnote: 15:58, pg. 1758.
4. Old Ironside: *Excerpt from This Day in History*, http://www.history.com/this-day-in-history/old-ironsides-earns-its-names
5. Dr. Joe Temple, *Like a Palm Tree*, http://www.livingbiblestudies.org/study/JT9/003.html, section: Palm Tree to be a Flourishing Tree.
6. Definition of flourish: http://biblesuite.com/hebrew/6524.htm.
7. William Dankenbring, *Mystery of the Olive Tree*, http://www.triumphpro.com/olive-tree-mystery.htm.

CHAPTER EIGHT:
1. Definition of demonstrate: synistemi, http://www.blueletterbible.org/lang/lexicon/lexicon. cfm?Strongs=G4921&t=KJV.
2. Shuwb: http://www.blueletterbible.org/lang/lexicon/lexicon.cfm?Strongs=H7725&t=KJV.
3. Definition of poor: http://www.blueletterbible.org/lang/lexicon/lexicon.cfm?Strongs=G4434&t=KJV.
4. Definition of marvelously: http://www.blueletterbible.org/lang/lexicon/lexicon.cfm?Strongs=H6381&t=KJV.
5. Definition of seek: http://www.blueletterbible.org/lang/lexicon/lexicon.cfm?Strongs=H1875&t=KJV.
6. Dr. Pardington, *Streams in the Desert*, (Grand Rapids, Michigan, Zondervan, Copyright 1925), pg. 355.
7. Definition for prosper: http://www.blueletterbible.org/lang/lexicon/lexicon.cfm?Strongs=H6743&t=KJV.
8. Natalie Grant, *The Desert Song*, Love Revolution.
9. C. Austin Miles (1868 – 1946), lyrics: *In the Garden*, RCA Victor Records catalog number LSP-1885.

CHAPTER NINE:
1. New International Version Study Bible, Zondervan, Footnote: pg. 1807.
2. Definition of humility: http://en.wikipedia.org/wiki/Humility.
3. Definition of walk: MacIntosh dictionary.
4. Sarah Young, *Jesus Calling*, (Nashville, Tennessee, Thomas Nelson Publishing, ©2004), January 25th, pg. 26.

CHAPTER TEN:
1. Martin Luther, http://www.goodreads.com/author/quotes/29874.Martin_Luther.
2. "I Wanna Be Like You (The Monkey Song)" is a song from Walt Disney's 1967 film, The Jungle Book. The song was sung by Louis Prima and written by songwriters Robert and Richard Sherman.
3. Harry Buschman, *The Man by the Window*, http://writers-voice.com/FGHIJ/H/Harry_Buschman_the_man_by_the_window.htm.
4. New International Version Study Bible, Zondervan, Footnote: Psalm 46:4, pg. 832.
5. Max Lucado, Cure for the Common Life, (Nashville, Tennessee, Thomas Nelson Publishing, 2005), pg. 3.

Annie Pajcic lives in Jacksonville, Florida with her husband and four children. Using her background in youth ministry, dance, and graphic design, she started ThouArtExalted in 2007. ThouArtExalted is a ministry using God's Word with the combination of art. When she doesn't have paint on her hands, she is writing and designing Bible studies, picking up kids, cooking dinner, or feeding the chickens. Visit her website at **www.thouartexalted.com** for art ideas, Bible studies, speaking engagements, service projects, and art blo**go**tionals. Check out her Facebook page at www.facebook.com/ThouArtExalted to see artwork in progress!

SPECIAL THANKS!

I had no idea where God would take Psalm One when He PLANTED this verse in my heart. Thank you Kellye Kunz for your excitement to start a Bible study and Deena Greene for asking for homework. Thank you to all the women who piloted the study and found my typos! Thank you to Lisa Lovelady, Heather Stoll, and Denise Fleming for your tireless edits. I also want to thank my parents, Anis and Barney Daley, who read each chapter with constructive advice and love. Thank you to my precious four—my prayer is that you will remain PLANTED all the days of your life. I especially want to thank my sweet husband, Curry, for his support, love, and encouragement to keep pursuing my God-given passions, step-by-step. I love you. And, to the Lord, You are my reason for being PLANTED. To YOU be the glory, forever. Amen.

NOTES:

NOTES:

MORE STUDIES BY THE AUTHOR!

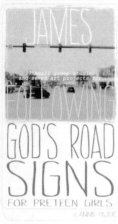

JAMES: One Year Curriculum for PRETEEN Girls and Boys

James: *Following God's Road Signs* is a 27-week Bible study on the book of James for middle school girls and boys. It is written to encourage and deepen your faith when life isn't quite so easy. But God is on your side and gives you INSTRUCTIONS for how to navigate— even when you choose to drive your OWN way often finding yourself on dead-end streets. The book of James is a road map guiding you in the right direction. *Following God's Road Signs* teaches you to put your FAITH INTO ACTION by stopping, looking at God's map, and asking HIM for directions. This study is great for Youth Groups, Small Groups, and Homeschool Groups.

What You Get:
- Study The Book Of James Verse-By-Verse In A Fun, Creative & Preteen-Friendly Way
- 27 Exciting Bible Lessons
- Creative Art Projects
- Dig-Deep Discussion Questions
- Lessons Come In a **Digital PDF** Format For Easy Sharing

Creative Art Projects Included!

JOURNAL WITH ME: MOTHER/DAUGHTER DEVOTIONAL

JOURNAL with ME is a Bible study/devotional for mothers with preteen and teenage daughters. The study focuses on **six** verses in Philippians designed for you to grow deeper in God's Word and deeper in your relationship together. ONE *JOURNAL with ME* is shared as a mother/daughter team and then passed back and forth during the week to answer the devotional questions. Each lesson includes ONE or more of the following: a challenge, a memory verse, an art project or, a service idea to experience together.

VISIT: www.thouartexalted.com *for ordering information.*

Made in the USA
Columbia, SC
15 January 2018